Soul Journey

Also by Margaret Silf:

At Sea with God
Born to Fly
Daily Readings with Margaret Silf
Faith
Hidden Wings
Landmarks
Roots and Wings
Taste and See
The Miller's Tale and Other Parables
The Other Side of Chaos
Wayfaring

All published by Darton, Longman and Todd

Soul Journey

with scripture and story towards the best we can be

MARGARET SILF

DARTON · LONGMAN + TODD

First published in Great Britain in 2020 by
Darton, Longman and Todd Ltd
1 Spencer Court
140–142 Wandsworth High Street
London SW18 4JJ

ISBN 978-0-232-53442-9

A catalogue record for this book is available from the British Library.

Designed and produced by Judy Linard

Contents

Looking forward

The day begins well. The prospect is full of promise. We are going on a hike and already we can see in the distance the mountain we are hoping to climb. We can see the whole mountain, neatly framed between earth and sky. The road ahead looks clear and easy.

We gradually get closer to the start of our hike. Now the way ahead doesn't seem quite so obvious. We can't see the whole mountain any more. We see other hikers ahead of us, struggling up the rocky outcrops. We get closer still and now we can see only the steep slope of one flank of the mountainside. It looks quite formidable. We begin to wonder how we can possibly begin to scale it.

And eventually we are right up to the foot of the mountain, and now all we can see is a rockface. Surely there is no way anyone can climb that. But we haven't come this far to give up now. We begin to climb, taking a few tentative steps, and only then do we notice narrow trails. Maybe they are just sheep tracks, but they convince us to keep going, and to find our own path up the mountain.

The spiritual journey is very much like this. It looks so obvious and easy from a distance – a beautiful mountain that so many have climbed before us. But the closer we approach, the harder it looks, until we are on the rockface and realise that we will have to make our own trail. with His will first

The image of a mountain has often been used to suggest an ascent to higher things, a spiritual quest to come closer to God. Our mountain on this particular journey is about both of those things, but it is, very specifically, about growing towards the best we can be, both as individuals and as all humankind. This quest can be compared to a mountain because it costs effort, patience and determination to keep going, and in particular it requires of us two things: the humility to recognise that we are at present far from the best we can be, either personally or collectively; and the trust that we can be so much more. It isn't a guilt trip, to obsess over our failures, but a journey of hope and faith that with every step we take, we can move closer to our best – our most fully human – selves.

As we begin this six-week journey it may feel as though we have it all mapped out, but experience reminds us that as we actually live each day, anything can happen, and our best-laid plans may fall apart. Or maybe the way ahead already feels like an impenetrable rock-face with no apparent way forward. If so, be reassured by the experience of many who have gone before us and discovered that there is a way, and that we find it as we walk, trusting that the next step will become clear as we go. We also find that we are not alone. We have a guide who calls himself the Way and we have many companions who like us are also making their own trails up the holy mountain.

This particular hike is a journey through the season of Lent. Perhaps you are very familiar with the Christian calendar, and you have kept the Lenten season all your life. If so, you will easily recognise the pattern of the journey ahead of us, following the days and weeks from Ash Wednesday, through Lent and Holy Week to Easter Sunday. If you are a spiritual pilgrim with no affiliation to the established churches, and the shape of the traditional six-week Lenten period is less familiar, the journey ahead is an opportunity to follow your quest for a deeper spirituality. All are welcome on this journey. There are no exclusions or pre-conditions.

Whether you see yourself as an ambler, a rambler or an Olympic mountaineer, this is your soul journey. May it surprise you, revitalise you, challenge you and reveal fresh horizons that will always beckon you beyond yourself towards your better and your very best self. Trust that every step towards our best that each one of us takes is also a step for all of us. Let your soul lead the way because your soul knows the Guide.

A word of thanks ...

The journey we make is not a solitary one. We make it with each other. We are way-companions for each other. Nor is the journey that leads to the publication of a book a solitary one, but a team undertaking. My very warmest thanks go especially to David Moloney, Helen Porter and Judy Linard at Darton, Longman and Todd, for all your encouragement, your professional expertise and your personal engagement that together have brought *Soul Journey* into being. I hope you know how much I have appreciated the ongoing gift of your friendship and guidance through all the years we have worked together.

Finally, and by no means least, I thank all my personal way-companions, those still walking the trail and those who have travelled beyond the horizon, especially the late Gerard Hughes SJ. To each and every one of you I wish *Buen Camino, Guten Weg*, and '*may the road rise to meet you*'.

MARGARET SILF

ASH WEDNESDAY TO THE
FIRST SUNDAY IN LENT

Setting Out

ASH WEDNESDAY
Life seasons

There is a season for everything,
a time for every occupation under heaven.
(Ecclesiastes 3:1)

If we wait for the right season to begin a journey we will probably never set out. This is true whether the journey is a change of direction in our outer life, or a deepening perspective on our inner life. It's so easy to find a reason to wait, until the perfect day arrives. Sometimes an external event can be the catalyst that gets us going. The tradition of undertaking a Lenten journey also offers us a reason and a season to venture more deeply into our spiritual life. Whether you are using this book during Lent or at any other time of the year, one thing is true. Today is the first day of the next stage of your soul journey.

The writer of Ecclesiastes has given us a memorable phrase, often used in many different contexts. *For everything there is a season.* What does this observation tell us about the nature of the journey ahead of us? What spiritual seasons might we recognise, and what season is currently governing our hearts and minds?

There's a season for building things up, and a season for letting things go. Both are good and necessary at different times of our life. Generally speaking, the first half of life is the season of acquiring, building up, growing and expanding, and the second half of life urges us to let go of much that we have acquired, in a natural process of emptying.

There's a season for fighting battles, and a season for

retreating from the fray and conserving our energy for more important matters. There's a season for throwing ourselves heart and soul into new projects and adventures, and there's a season for resting quietly and reflecting on our experience.

There's a time for actively protesting about the state of the world, and a time for standing back and recognising what we can and cannot change and seeking the wisdom to know the difference. A time for saving the world and a time for reflecting on what changes need to happen in ourselves. A time for speaking out, and a time for keeping quiet.

In every life there are seasons of rejoicing – over new life, a new relationship, a new home, a new job – and seasons of grieving for a lost love, a missed opportunity, a broken heart.

Every life knows many seasons. We know our springtime, when a limitless future stretches ahead of us. We know our summertime, when the blossom fades but our life's fruitfulness is taking shape. We know the mellow light of harvest time, when our life's day is growing shorter, but the fruits are being gathered and stored. And then comes winter. The season of dying back and the time for facing wind and cold, yet knowing that beneath the frozen earth fresh life is quietly sleeping.

The spiritual landscape also has its seasons. There are times of unquestioning faith in the ways of God and times of disturbing doubt. There are times when the river of faith runs clear and bright and times when it seems to dry up. There are times when we gladly seek the embrace of a faith community and times when we need to be alone to ponder the mystery as we search for our own deepest truth. There are times when we are vividly aware of the presence of the Holy and times when we have no felt sense of the presence of God.

I am now in the later stages of my life, and mindful of the need for some radical de-cluttering, to save my family a painful task when I leave the world. In the course of this process I have shredded seven volumes of my own spiritual journals and passed the result to my friend who rescues old chickens from battery farms to offer them a contented retirement in her garden when their 'useful' life is over. My journals now provide comfortable bedding for these veterans, and there is something that feels profoundly right about that. For one thing it means that no one except the chickens will ever read them, but it has also given me the opportunity to browse through what I have written through the years and to realise that issues that completely dominated my thoughts and prayers in the past and kept me awake at night, banging on God's door in search of a resolution, have passed by now like water under a bridge, finding their own untangling, and allowing me to move on in my life.

As we welcome the flow of memory may we also welcome the legacy of all the seasons of our lives, both the harsh and the gentle, knowing that the Way is greater than all of those who walk it, and is guided by safer hands.

Pause ...

.... to ask for the grace to notice the various seasons of our lives, gratefully receiving their fruits and to recognise where we find ourselves right now.

THURSDAY
A star in the east

And see, the star they had seen at its rising went before them until it halted over the place where the child was. Seeing the star, they rejoiced with very great joy, and going into the house they saw the child with Mary, his mother, and falling down they worshipped him. Then, opening their treasure chests, they offered him gifts of gold and frankincense and myrrh.'
(Matthew 2:9-11)

The three wise men have appeared in every Nativity play in Christendom, in their dressing gowns and paper crowns. I particularly remember one such drama at my granddaughter's nursery, in which there were three and a half wise men, two of whom were wise ladies. The 'half' was a disgruntled little brother determined not to be left out. Everyone wants to be a wise pilgrim journeying to the unknown destination where great treasure will be discovered. Meanwhile the star graces the topmost branches of our Christmas trees, but is rarely glimpsed during the dark nights through which our soul's journey inevitably leads us.

Just a story, consigned now to the dusty shelves of childhood nostalgia? Or perhaps something more profound than we can imagine? Our hope for a guiding light to give us direction in a directionless world? Our hope that the journey might be leading us to something *more* than simply striving and surviving? Some destiny that would make us fall to our knees before the sheer wonder of it all?

A thank you card for a teacher recently caught my eye. It had a picture of a plant flourishing in the sunlight and the greeting read 'Thank you for helping me to grow.' When I look back I discover my own personal constellation of people who have influenced me through the years and helped me to grow, and I am sincerely grateful to them. A good way to engage more deeply with our soul journey is to take time to remember these real and personal stars, and maybe also to thank them, if this is still possible.

But there is another guiding star that may surprise you. It's the star of *desire*. Who would think that desire might be a reliable guide? Isn't desire something we should be wary of, something that might seduce us into dangerous paths? Well perhaps it depends on the *depth* of the desire. At the deepest level, the magi desired to discover the new life whose birth the star announced. Any other, more superficial, desires, such as staying comfortably at home, or pursuing attractive diversions, were eclipsed by the one overriding desire to make the journey that would lead to their true heart's desire. We see the same kind of overriding desire expressed in the lives, for example, of parents who make enormous sacrifices of energy, resources and personal freedom to give their children the best possible start in life.

To follow the star of our deepest desire can mean many things. It can be about recognising our personal gifts and working to bring them to fruition, being willing to go without some of the lesser wants and wishes that might distract us. It can mean loving another person so much that we freely give them the best of our time and attention, and in doing so discover that this is also what makes us feel more alive and fulfilled ourselves. It can mean being so passionate about an issue that affects all our lives that we dedicate ourselves to further that cause, because the greater good matters more to us than our personal comfort.

Frederick Buechner expresses it like this: '*The place God calls you to is the place where your deep gladness and the world's deep hunger meet*'. It isn't about suppressing our desires, but about discovering where those desires match up with something that the world needs, and once that match is made, new possibilities come to birth. We feel most at peace with ourselves and with each other when we follow the star of our very deepest desire and discover that it leads us to a simple stable in our hearts where all that is best in us is just coming to birth.

We have nothing to bring to that place but our gifts. The gold of our own unique treasure, that gift that we alone can bring to the world. The frankincense that overwhelms us with its sweet fragrance of awe and wonder at all that is coming to pass in ourselves and in our world. And the myrrh that reminds us of the cost of this journey, and that both rain and sunlight, tears and joy are necessary to make the rainbow.

Pause....

... to ask for the grace to trust our brightest guiding star even, and especially, when the night is at its darkest.

FRIDAY
No maps

*I shall lead the blind by a road they do not know,
by paths they do not know I shall guide them.
I shall turn the darkness before them into light
and the rough places into level ground.
(Isaiah 42:16)*

We're going a journey. We might assume that an important part of what we need will be a map. And we might be in for a surprise.

Of course there is no shortage of spiritual maps, each proposing that we take a particular route on our soul's journey. Some are more insistent than others. Some are lists of absolute rules, while others are more in the nature of friendly suggestions, leaving us to take responsibility for the way we travel. But how helpful are they, and can we really rely on them to guide us through this uncharted territory?

I met an elderly gentleman once who had been a mountain guide, responsible for leading hikers along safe trails through the local hills. It was fascinating to hear what skills were required. Of course mountain guides need to be able to read maps accurately and to administer first aid if necessary, but I would not have imagined, for example, that they also need to be able to guide a rescue helicopter to a safe landing place. All in all, getting accreditation was a tough call, and involved both written and practical examinations.

On the day of his practical test, he had to guide a group of hikers through unfamiliar terrain, for which he was given a map. The examiner was among the hikers, but the candidate didn't know his identity. The hike was going well until the guide realised that the map no longer appeared to match the terrain through which they were walking. He assumed he must have missed a turning somewhere, and if so, he would have failed the accreditation test. Now, however, the priority was to get the hikers safely back to base, and he needed to navigate the terrain through which they were actually walking. The map had outlived its usefulness.

They all returned safely. The examiner approached the candidate, who of course was waiting to be told he had failed the test. In fact, quite the opposite happened. 'Congratulations,' the examiner smiled his approval. 'We deliberately gave you a faulty map. The test was to see what you would do when you realised that the map didn't match the actual terrain. You reacted correctly, by focusing on the terrain, and letting go of any dependence on the map.'

This story resonated deeply with the story of my spiritual journey. At first there was no serious discrepancy between the official map and my own spiritual landscape. In time, however, I found that the map was answering questions that I wasn't asking, and was not too helpful in providing any answers to my real questions. I've learned for myself that, like the mountain guide, I need to walk the terrain I'm actually in, my own real-life situations and relationships with all their awkward twists and turns, and not try to follow a one-size-fits-all map. And it's about navigating the landscape where I really am, and not where I wish I were, or where I, or other people, think I ought to be, or where I might have been if I'd started from somewhere else.

Many people are finding that the spiritual maps, or the rules and methods they were taught as children, no longer help them navigate the real issues of contemporary life. This is not to suggest that we should throw out the maps, but rather that we might regard them as a starting point, giving us an overview of the journey our souls are undertaking, but not able to chart the unique and personal shape of our own lives, which, of course, is changing and evolving with every step we take, and in every relationship and interaction in which we engage as we travel.

It may well dismay us to know that there is no map for the personal intricacies of our soul journey, but the promise in Isaiah turns such dismay on its head. It is the *blind,* we learn, who are the ones who are guided, and it is the paths that are *unknown* that are to be explored. This is deeply reassuring, given that I have no idea where my journey is heading, and I can't see even the next mile of the path. Even if I could see the path I wouldn't recognise it because it is completely unknown – and unknowable. It is the tomorrow that today can never see coming. The promise goes on to say that light will follow on this darkness and the rough terrain will be levelled. Not a map, but a vision, and I'll gladly settle for that.

Pause ...

... to ask for the grace to trust the guide who leads us in our blindness and takes us safely along paths we do not know.

SATURDAY
A very early scan

My dear friends, we are already God's children,
but what we shall be has not yet been revealed.
(1 John 3:2)

When I received the email from my daughter, telling me they were expecting their first child, I was sitting at a stranger's desk in an office in Sydney, Australia. She had attached an image of a very early scan of the newly-conceived baby. I don't know how long I sat there, simply gazing at this speck of life who was my granddaughter. The scan told me she was 6mm long, just a cluster of cells you might say, but I knew from that moment on that this tiny scrap of life was already my grandchild, and would always be so, even should the pregnancy, for any reason, fail to result in a live birth.

You'd have to be a trained medic to see the image of a real child in an early ultrasound scan. Even in later pregnancy the outline of the foetus is not easy to recognise, though a trained eye might be able to tell the gender of the coming life. There are sophisticated later scans in 3-D that give you a rather clearer image, but even this is more in the nature of an 'artist's impression'. Nothing prepares you for the real thing, when you hold the baby in your arms and feel both the joy and the huge responsibility of your new role as a parent.

And nothing prepares you for the struggle that will be involved in bringing this child to birth. Not for nothing is the place where this frequently happens called the Labour Ward. And the child's arrival is only the start of a long, uphill journey as you embark on the mammoth task of raising your little one through all the challenges of childhood and adolescence to full maturity.

Paul writes of our human spiritual journey in these same terms: 'We know that the whole creation, until this time, has joined together in groaning and labour pains' (Romans 8:22).

Well this would certainly account for all the distress and pain we experience in our lives and in the world. It can feel like one long and anguished struggle. Life in the Labour Ward feels like that too, and yet we know that this is a journey that for most (though tragically not for all) ends with the emergence of a new human life.

What about the labour pains of all creation that Paul mentions? Can we trust that these too are the precursors of new life? Is anything coming to birth in our human story, or is it all just a series of random events, as some would suggest? The French priest-palaeontologist, Pierre Teilhard de Chardin is convinced that humanity is engaged in a process of spiritual, as well as physical evolution. He suggests that in every choice we make we are either helping this process to progress more closely to the best we can be or causing it to regress. He sees the destiny of our evolution as a higher state of consciousness in which we will be, in the words of Irenaeus, 'human beings fully alive', and fully reflecting the glory of God. If we want to see what this looks like in a human life, we need only contemplate the life of Jesus of Nazareth. However, living our lives in mindfulness of our choices and their consequences is never going to be easy. There will be many times when we feel we are taking two steps backward for every step forward. Which is quite a good description of how it feels to be in the first stage of labour, striving and straining to bring a baby into the world.

St Paul also, memorably, reminds us that 'now we see in a mirror, confusedly, but then we shall see face to face' (1 Corinthians 13:12).

He might have been looking at an ultrasound scan of an unborn child when he wrote that. All I could see on that screen in Sydney was a hazy reflection of what might possibly develop into a recognisable child. Who she would become was a complete mystery. Now I see her face to face, and as her life continues to unfold, I discover more and more about the unique wonder of her being. And like every other child, and adult, she is a child of God, but what she will be in the future has not yet been revealed.

Pause ...

... to ask for the grace to trust that we are evolving into more than we can imagine, even though we can only see the haziest reflection of all that we are called to become.

SABBATH PAUSE
Let your soul catch up

'Be still, and know that I am God.'
(Psalm 46:11)

We change gear now, and make a sabbath pause to reflect over the journey so far.

A story is told of a group of Western explorers making an expedition into a remote jungle area, accompanied by a group of local guides who knew the terrain and were willing to carry the explorers' equipment.

As is customary in Western undertakings, there was a detailed schedule and a tight timescale. After an initial briefing, they all set off, and they travelled together for three days. Everything was going very well, the explorers thought. If they could keep up this pace they would meet their deadline.

But on the fourth day, when they gathered for an early morning start, there was no sign of the local guides. A search revealed that they were sitting resting in a shady spot, quietly contemplating life. When challenged, they stated simply: 'We have marched for three days and we have met your schedule. Now it is time for us to rest and let our souls catch up with us.'

And this is what we will do as we make this Lenten journey. Each Sunday we will pause to let our souls catch up with us, as we take stock of the week's journey.

One way to come to inner stillness is to focus on a few words of scripture, entering into them deeply and contemplatively using the time-honoured method of *lectio divina*. This approach to prayer involves reading – slowly and thoughtfully – a short piece of scripture and noticing what suggests itself to you, especially any ways in which the words connect to what is going on in your life. Keep repeating the reading, letting the words soak into you, until you have found your own 'nugget' of meaning for the day. You might like to try meditating in this way with the psalmist's words: 'Be still, and know that I am God.'

As you reflect on the journey we have made over the past four days, the following pointers might be useful. Take any that help you, and let go of all the rest. Stay with what is drawing you closer to your own deep centre, where God is indwelling.

- What season prevails in your heart at present? Is it the flush of springtime or the steady growth of summer, the ripeness of autumn or the cold of winter?
- What spiritual season are you living through: how is the balance between faith and doubt?
- When you reflect on the desires that motivate you, where do you locate your deepest desire? What star is guiding you to the new life coming to birth in you? What gifts will you bring to that inner 'stable'?
- What guiding stars would you like to see directing humanity as a whole? Which of our shared values do you consider most important for the future of our species and our planet and for the human soul?
- What maps have guided your journey in the past? Do they still reflect the actual landscape of your life? How do you feel when you think about walking your spiritual journey without a formal map, trusting only in the promise that you will be guided precisely in your blindness, and that the tomorrow you fear today will open up trails both radically new and utterly trustworthy.
  The poet Keats speaks of what he calls 'negative capability', which means the ability to be in a state of not knowing, but open to a future that can never be precisely defined. It is a quality that frees us of our human compulsion to pin

things down in every detail, which in turn frees us of our insistent need to control things. How do you feel about this state of being still unformed, like an unborn child, only recognisable in the hazy outline of an ultrasound scan?

- How do you feel about the suggestion that humanity is in a process of spiritual evolution? How might you become more aware of how your own choices may be advancing this process or holding it back?
- Where do you see any signs that humanity is evolving spiritually towards a better version of who we can be collectively? Is there any way you can personally contribute to this positive growth? How can you personally grow towards the best you can be?

In these early days we have taken stock of our starting point. Next week we will reflect on some of the invitations issued in scripture to trust the journey and to set out.

FIRST WEEK OF LENT

Invitations

MONDAY
Burning bushes

'Remove the sandals from your feet,
for the place where you are standing is holy ground.'
(Exodus 3:5)

Traditionally, Lent begins with ashes, sometimes administered metaphorically in exhortations to penance, sometimes physically in the form of a sign on the forehead. If you are making this journey through the season of Lent, it may surprise you that this first full week should begin not with a lament of *mea culpa* but with a moment of speechless amazement.

The story of the burning bush is very familiar. We heard it at school, and we probably drew pictures of it when we were five. It has certainly made its mark and the account of it in Exodus begins by telling us that Moses, the recipient of this dramatic vision, was quietly minding his own business at the time, looking after the flock of his father-in-law Jethro, near Horeb on 'the far side of the desert'.

A common assumption is that 'ordinary' folk don't see burning bushes, and most of us are not out in the desert tending our father-in-law's flock. But just hold it there. I remember a moment when I was meditating on this incident and I suddenly realised that I was indeed spending much of my time and energy attending to the needs of my father-in-law's 'flock', namely his son and grandchild and other members of the tribe, and that there were certainly days when this could feel like 'the far side of the desert'. Whatever your personal family circumstances may be, you almost certainly have a 'flock' to tend in some form or another. You and Moses already have a connection.

31

As for burning bushes. Surely this is just a picture from an ancient text, hardly likely to be replicated in the High Street? This is the stuff of theatrical drama and Hollywood movies. Moses sees this bush on fire, for no apparent reason, in the middle of nowhere, and goes to investigate. Though the bush is on fire it isn't being consumed by the flames, so whatever this fire is about, it is not something destructive. It is, however, very much an invitation and one it would be hard to ignore. Helpfully, it speaks to him, inviting him personally to recognise this as a holy encounter, and to behave accordingly, by taking off his sandals.

A friend recently sent me a short video showing various scenes from the natural world in which the photographer had seen something more – perhaps the sudden shaft of sunlight that lights up a dark forest or the wide eyes of a child watching the waves break on the shore – and had captured the moment on camera. Gerard Manley Hopkins describes this way of perceiving the world as the ability to see the *inscape* of things, the heart of the matter that makes you gasp and pause, and stand and stare, and – yes – take off your shoes, because suddenly you see just how amazing creation actually is. Mostly we tend to see the world around us in the usual three dimensions, but there are moments when suddenly we see a deeper dimension in which, as Hopkins declares, 'the world is charged with the grandeur of God', shimmering and quivering with a life of its own.

My own burning bushes include an evening in winter when I was seven and saw – *really saw* – the stars, the infinity of them, their immense beauty, and their reminder that though I was a mere wisp of life on a tiny planet, I was part of it all. There are not so many bushes in my story – I could probably count them on my fingers, but they have penetrated my soul and changed me for ever. They came so silently and gently, but with the power to shock me into a whole new orbit of perception

Regrettably we live in an age of celebrity culture today, and the glare of neon lights can easily appear to eclipse the galaxies. The latest very flawed and human stars that flicker across our large, small and phone-sized screens, can dominate our consciousness but they will never make us want to take off our sandals.

There is an image on the internet of a photo taken at the site that claims to be the location of the original burning bush in the grounds of St Catherine's Monastery in the Sinai desert. The photo reveals a fire extinguisher standing beside it! Please don't be tempted to dowse your own burning bushes with cynicism or scepticism. They are infinitely precious, personally-given conduits of divine energy.

Pause ...

... to ask for the grace to keep returning to our own burning bushes and take off our sandals in recognition of the holy ground on which we stand.

TUESDAY
Life welcomes life

'As soon as your greeting reached my ears,
the child in my womb leapt for joy.'
(Luke 1:44)

When Mary of Nazareth discovered she was pregnant, and went to visit her cousin Elizabeth in the hill country of Judah, the mood would surely have been anxious. Forget the Christmas card images of a young girl radiating joy that she is carrying a very special child. Try, instead, to imagine how she might really have been feeling. This totally unexpected and unplanned pregnancy turns everything on its head. How do you tell your parents that you had a vision of an angel and now you are pregnant? How do you tell the man to whom you are engaged that there is a child on the way, and you can't account for where it came from? How do you face the crowds who quite legally can stone you to death when they get to hear about your plight?

It can't have been easy for Elizabeth either, carrying her own unexpected child when she thought she had safely navigated the menopause. Where would she get the energy, at her age, to raise a child? How would it affect her marriage? How would it be when the child became a teenager and she would be an old woman?

Very understandably, Mary, seeking a brief respite from the very pressing problems that lie ahead of her, makes her way to her cousin's home and a woman-to-woman talk. If anyone can help her deal with this dilemma, Elizabeth might. She desperately needs someone who will understand and be there for her. She needs a bolthole and a listening ear.

Quite often, for us too, it is in a time of crisis that we feel the impulse to embark on a deeper spiritual journey, and to seek out a special kind of companionship along the way.

Elizabeth, you might think, would be able to offer good advice about the difficult relationship problems this pregnancy is causing for her younger cousin, and she might even have wise words on childcare issues, but that isn't what is recorded about their conversation. Instead it is the unborn children who steal the show. Each mother-to-be recognises a stirring of the new life she is carrying in response to the new life her cousin is carrying. The babies greet each other *in utero*. Life greets life with an unmistakable strong and silent fluttering as the unborn John greets the unborn Jesus.

Sometimes the invitation of the Holy Spirit to embark on a deeper soul journey can feel as fleeting and fragile as the stirring of an unborn child. Something deep within us is calling us towards a fuller meaning and expression of life. The joy of this experience is amplified when we sense a resonance with the corresponding inner joy of another human being. The as yet unborn life in ourselves greets the as yet unborn life in the other. This happens especially when we share something of our spiritual journey with a trusted companion – the Celts had a name for such a relationship; they called it the bond of the *anam cara*, or soul friend.

A friend of mine touring Britain by bike was making a journey from Cumbria down to South Yorkshire. As he pedalled his way up and down the northern hills, he began to feel weary. Another cyclist overtook him on the road and noticed that he was flagging. He slowed down and asked, 'You seem to be a bit weary. Would it help if I cycled alongside you, making the pace and keeping you company for a while?' The offer was gratefully accepted, and they rode together for several miles. The second cyclist suggested that they should stop for a little break and a cup of tea, and when it came to the point where he would have turned off the road to go to his own destination, he continued instead for a further ten miles to help his companion find the right road.

Soul friendship is a bit like this. It provides companionship and encouragement, even suggesting possibilities for rest and revitalisation along the journey, and gladly walking the extra mile when needed. It is one of the ways in which the source of all life invites us to nourish the growth of that inner life in each other.

In Celtic Christian times it was assumed that anyone who was seriously making a spiritual journey would have such a travelling companion. Perhaps you would appreciate such companionship as you embark on your journey? You may find the right companion close to home: it would be someone you trust absolutely, someone who will listen to your story with warmth and empathy, helping you notice the movements of the Spirit in your life, without trying to 'direct' or 'correct' you. It has been wisely said that 'when the pilgrim is ready, the guide appears', and so far this piece of wisdom has never failed me.

Pause ...

... to ask for the grace to recognise and welcome all that is coming to birth in ourselves and in each other and to be open to receiving and offering soul-companionship along the way.

WEDNESDAY
Trailmaking

A voice of one crying in the desert,
'Prepare a way for the Lord,
make his paths straight.'
(Matthew 3:3)

Not everyone expects a spiritual journey to include an invitation to become a road-builder. It sounds like a far cry from praying quietly in the parish church or engaging in a spiritual retreat. Frankly it sounds more like hard work than an invitation. Yet this phrase, urging us to 'prepare a way for the Lord' has taken on a life of its own, not least through the seventies' musical *Godspell*.

It would be a good idea to check out the job description before we decide how to respond. How do we imagine 'a way for the Lord'? Some might see it as a motorway. It has to be solid and straight and everyone has to get onto it and drive according to the rules. Others imagine a narrow winding track, not easy to find and even harder to walk, which is more in line with the glimpse given in the gospels where Matthew advises us that 'it is a narrow gate and a hard road that leads to life, and only a few find it' (Matthew 7:14).

In spite of this rather disconcerting summing-up, there is no questioning John the Baptist's enthusiasm in urging us, nevertheless, to take part in preparing a way. We need to let go of the motorway idea however, whatever the protests of those who construct religious highways and seek to direct the traffic. The 'narrow way' looks rather different. Narrow ways are usually best travelled in single file, though we might reasonably hope for lay-bys where a few pilgrims can gather to share their experience of the journey. On such narrow trails there is no room for five-star hotels or corporate headquarters.

How might we actively prepare such ways? One suggestion is that we prepare a way for the Lord by the way we walk our own trail through life. Every time we make a choice that adds to the store of love, hope, trust and integrity in the world, we help to make the way a little clearer for those who follow after.

The way in question is the Lord's, however, and not ours, and the best way we can help to prepare it is to avoid clogging it up with obstructions of our own making and rendering it more difficult for others to travel. I used to think my life was like a kind of parcel with a beginning and an end and my hope would be that my life-parcel would eventually be sufficiently acceptable to get me through the pearly gates. Then I realised that life is more like an open channel– a collection of circumstances, situations and relationships through which the Holy Spirit seeks to flow with healing and life-giving power. My task is not to manufacture an acceptable parcel, but to avoid blocking the flow of the Spirit.

When the Berlin Wall fell in 1989 most of it was used to make road-making material, and the Germans, who know a lot about making roads, say that it made some of the best material ever. The Wall, that had been a barrier for 28 cruel years, dividing friends and families, now became a means of re-connection.

This fact was a source of great inspiration to me. I lived myself in the shadow of the Berlin Wall for three years during the Cold War and I knew, at first hand, what an intractable and brutal obstruction it was. Its transformation into highways helps me to trust that the issues that obstruct the flow of the Spirit through our own lives can also be transformed, in God's hands, into channels of grace. Nothing is wasted in the divine economy, and our stumbling blocks can become stepping stones that facilitate a way for the Lord.

Will we join the traffic jam on the man-made religious highways with their pre-defined destinations, or dare we trust that 'a way for the Lord' is actually being laid down in the trails of our own journeys, with all the twists and turns that they bring? There is no path until we walk it. We make the way as we walk. We don't know where it leads because until we walk it, there is no path. Paths are made when we place one foot in front of the other and dare to walk on, without needing to know the destination. Each step is a choice we make, a word we speak, an action we undertake. Each step will either help to take us a little closer to the best we can be, or it will hinder that goal.

There are as many trails leading through the wilderness of life as there are pilgrims trying to walk that wilderness. Each trail is one unique opportunity to prepare a way for the Lord. The American poet-philosopher, Ralph Waldo Emerson, expresses it like this:

'Do not go where the path may lead, go instead where there is no path and leave a trail.'

Pause ...

... to ask for the grace to let each step we take today be taken in the light of our deepest integrity and under the guidance of the Holy Spirit, trusting that when we do so, we are helping to prepare a way for the Lord.

THURSDAY
The cloak of prophecy

*Leaving there, Elijah came on Elisha son of Shaphat as he
was ploughing behind twelve yoke of oxen, he himself being
with the twelfth. Elijah passed near to him and threw his
cloak over him. Elisha left his oxen and ran after Elijah.*
(1 Kings 19:19)

Some are born prophets, some become prophets, some have
the cloak of prophecy thrust upon them. Elisha clearly belongs
in the last category. It may seem an improbable method of
inviting someone to be a prophet. The description in *Kings*
conjures up visions of Elijah going in search of the person
whom he (or God) has chosen to be his successor, patiently
waiting for the unsuspecting Elisha to pass by, and then
throwing his cloak over him. Such a scene might not be out of
place in a *Harry Potter* story.

The cloak is a mantle of power – in this case, the power of
the prophet. A prophet, in the Old Testament, was regarded
as a representative of God, charged with communicating God's
message to the people. The prophet's authority came straight
from God. So this is one of the more insistent invitations that
might arise on a soul journey. Surely not, you may protest. We
can't exactly imagine ourselves striding the land proclaiming
God's truth, especially given that many who claim to do that in
our own times are actually more concerned with proclaiming
their own agendas. We have become rather cynical about self-
styled prophets and may be in danger of missing the real thing
when we encounter him or her.

Nevertheless, there are two aspects of this story that

are very relevant to our spiritual journeying. The first is the question of our own invitation to receive the cloak of prophecy. The second is the question of tradition.

A prophet articulates the message of God, but this doesn't have to be a call to the nations issued from the mountaintops. Everyday prophets are all around us. Parents teaching their children the difference between truth and falsehood. Young people demanding urgent action to mitigate the effects of climate change. Political activists campaigning on behalf of the most vulnerable in our society. Anyone who boldly speaks truth to power, or honestly, humbly and authentically stands up for the values that define what it means to be a fully human being is a true inheritor of the cloak of prophecy.

I've always been fascinated by the second vivid image, of Elisha ploughing the field behind twelve teams of oxen. For me this is a powerful reminder that our own soul journey is not something undertaken in isolation but is part of a long continuum of spiritual journeying. I reflect gratefully on my personal 'teams of oxen'. These are those significant soul companions who have walked the path, and ploughed the furrows of faith ahead of me. They are individuals who have shown me, through their own lives, what it means to choose the path of integrity in every situation. Some of them died long before I was born, others are still young. Some are familiar to us all, others are known only to me and to their own close circles.

When I walk among my twelve teams of oxen, I find mentors whose particular wisdom has shaped my life choices. I find elders, in my own family and beyond, who have modelled what it means to live the best life you can live, even though they never knew the influence they were having. I find those who spoke their truth with courage in the face of opposition and helped me to be a little less timid, and others who kept silence amid the storms and taught me when and how to keep the peace.

All of them remind me that just as we are indebted to all who have gone ahead of us, so we have a responsibility to those who follow after. Whatever prophetic 'cloak' has been passed to us, we pass on to others in the future, if only by the way we make our choices and communicate some small glimpse of truth and integrity in our own lives. There are countless ways of passing on the messages of Life and Truth and some of them come as personal invitations to each of us.

The cloak of prophecy is a powerful invitation. We are free to accept it or refuse it, and the invitation will be repeated in many different ways as we walk the highways and by-ways of our lives.

Picasso once remarked that 'tradition is having a baby, not wearing your grandfather's hat'. Some see tradition as something static, an unchanging model of how things should be, like the way grandad wore his hat, but a journey is something dynamic. We honour tradition most fully when we apply the finest of the values that have been passed down to us to the situations of the twenty-first century.

Pause ...

... to ask for the grace to find and embrace our place in the long continuum of faith and prophecy and to live true to the invitation that is given to us in our own personal form of Elijah's cloak

FRIDAY
Deeper water

When Jesus had finished speaking, he said to Simon,
'Put out into deep water and pay out your nets for a catch.'
(Luke 5:4)

It had been quite a morning for Simon Peter. It began as usual, as he quietly got on with his life, cleaning his nets and contemplating the day ahead. An itinerant preacher was addressing the large crowds gathering along the shore. Peter listened with one ear, as he worked, and then the unthinkable happened. Jesus came right up to him and stepped into his boat.

I would love to know what Peter said at this point, or even what he thought, but this remains forever shrouded in mystery, and we hear, instead, what Jesus had to say: 'Put out into deep water.'

I spent a memorable holiday many years ago on the south coast of Turkey. A gradually shelving sandy beach gave way to warm inviting water. It was easy to linger in the shallows, letting the water lap around my feet. But the call to go deeper grew louder, and soon I ventured further until the water reached my waist. The water's invitation was very gentle, insistent but not coercive. It allowed me to take my own time and choose my own pace as it gradually drew me to the deeper reaches of the ocean. And once I had passed the final breaker line, I found myself in water that was deep enough for swimming. I was out of my depth. I surrendered myself to the buoyancy of the ocean and experienced the joy of a very different kind of engagement with the water.

I've found that the spiritual journey follows a similar pattern. First, we paddle in the shallows, and only when we are ready does the deeper water call us. In the deeper water we are no longer in control or reliant on our own strength. We have come up against our own limitations. We have to trust the power of the greater mystery that holds us in being.

I can feel with Peter. I remember a time in my own life when it felt as though Jesus 'stepped into my boat', when I became more conscious of the invitation to be in a personal relationship with the holy mystery we call God. I remember the many years I spent paddling in the shallow waters of received faith and routine practice, and now I can see those times as a period of familiarisation with, and growing affection for, a community of fellow pilgrims. And then from that foundation, the call to go deeper, into those channels of faith that each of us must explore alone, though not unguided.

After calling Peter to put out into deeper water, Jesus then instructs him to lower the net, and the result is a huge catch of fish that almost breaks their nets. I certainly haven't reached those depths and never will, though I realise that each pilgrim's 'catch' is unique and serves a specific purpose, and that this isn't a competition. I can see, however, that you can't catch many fish if you don't risk putting out to sea. It is often remarked that you will never discover new lands if you don't leave the safety of the home harbour. This wisdom was confirmed for me when a seafaring friend told me that many of the magnificent yachts that occupy our coastal marinas never, in fact, go to sea. This fact stunned me somewhat. Why would you own a boat like that if you didn't intend to sail? Why would you be given the means to sail into deeper spiritual waters if all you wanted to do was paddle along the edge of the beach?

A soul journey is always a response to put out into deeper waters. And of course, there are sharks in the deep waters too. There are big questions with no easy answers. There are legitimate doubts. There are abuses of power in high places, and there is suffering and hardship among the little fish. All this awaits us in the deeper waters. We will encounter challenges not only about how we conduct our own lives, but how society functions, and how our country makes its choices and exercises its power in the world. The challenges will sometimes feel overwhelming, and we will, quite rightly, know that we are out of our depth.

And this is faith: to trust the ocean when we know we cannot fully trust ourselves.

Pause ...

... to ask for the grace to risk sailing our soul's boat into deep waters and for the courage to face whatever challenges those depths may hold, recognising the limitations of the boat and trusting the limitless power of the ocean.

SATURDAY

Sing a new song

O sing a new song to the Lord! Sing to the Lord, all the earth!
O sing to the Lord, bless his name!
(Psalm 96:1)

People who understand these things tell us that everyone can sing. I am not entirely convinced, but today the invitation is to sing – whether we think we can or not. It sounds like a very joyous invitation, and provided we are permitted to do our singing in the shower, surely an invitation that includes all of us, indeed 'all the earth' as the psalmist reminds us.

The Swedish film *As It Is in Heaven* tells the story of a professional musician and concert performer who has a heart attack and is advised to slow down, and retires to the sleepy Scandinavian village where he grew up. The local pastor soon notices his arrival and persuades him to take on the rather shaky church choir. Reluctantly he accepts the invitation and adopts a very unconventional approach to the task. He welcomes everyone – including those normally excluded because of various difficulties – and teaches them how to discover their own personal note. I questioned this at first, but when I tried it out, in the privacy of the bathroom, I realised that he's right. There is a particular natural note that we all have, and when we bring these together in community the result is – harmony! It's not just about music of course. It's an invitation to all of us to find our own personal way of participating in the human story, and if we do this, we will be responding to the psalmist's invitation to 'sing a new song'. Just for

46

information, the little choir in the film goes on to win first prize in an international choral festival.

Simply being invited to sing sounds daunting, especially to the shy and the stage-fearful. It happened to me when I was four, on holiday with an elderly relative, who found it acceptable to lift me up onto a makeshift stage on the beach to take part in a talent contest, in which I was forced to chirp my way through 'Jesus wants me for a sunbeam'. I think even Jesus might have gone off the idea if he heard my offering that day. My aversion to public performance was exacerbated even more when I was about six. I used to sing myself to sleep each night, until one evening my father, trying to get a bit of peace, called up to me to 'Stop pulling that cat's tail'. That was it. The end of any musical aspirations I might have had. (I should add that the 'cat' in question was purely hypothetical. I would never, even at that age, have pulled a real cat's tail.)

Sadly, it's a common experience today. Many people feel 'silenced'. Their voices are not being heard. This isn't just about the ability to sing. It's about the deep pain of not being included in the song of life. Those with the most strident voices dominate the music of the nations. The gentler undertones are drowned out by the cacophony of angry rhetoric.

So what does it mean, to 'sing a new song'? What if it has more to do with the music-maker than the instrument?

Our daughter married her South African husband in a chapel in the Drakensburg mountains. They asked a relative, who is a professor of church music, to play the organ for the ceremony, but there were two problems: the organ in the little chapel was considerably past its sell-by date and hadn't been tuned for years, and the professor was a perfectionist, used to playing the finest instruments.

However, he did his best, and we who were not so particular were happy to welcome the bridal pair to the accompaniment of Pachelbel's Canon. That the organist was gritting his teeth through the performance wasn't obvious to most people.

At the end of the service the pastor wished the couple

well and thanked all of us for coming. Then he turned to the impromptu organist and said: 'And a very special thankyou to you, sir, because today you have made that old organ *sing*.'

It was an unforgettable lesson to me that no matter how decrepit the instrument, the master musician can make it sing. No matter how inadequate we feel, we are all instruments through whom a new song can be sung if we accept the invitation from the master musician, acknowledging that the song doesn't depend on the state of the instrument, but the skill of the music-maker.

Pause ...

... to ask for the grace to find our own true note, our unique and indispensable part of the universal symphony, trusting that however untuned and inadequate we think we are, in the hands of the music-maker we are destined to sing a new song, along with all creation.

SABBATH PAUSE
Rest for your soul

*Come to me, all you who labour and are overburdened,
and I will give you rest. Take my yoke upon you and
learn from me, for I am gentle and humble in heart,
and you will find rest for your souls. For my yoke is
easy and my burden light.'*
(Matthew 11:28-30)

Time to take a sabbath pause again and reflect over what the
week has opened up for you. As you let these familiar words
from Matthew soak into your soul, I wonder how you are
really feeling. Look back over the past few days with their
demands, challenges and choices. Did the yoke feel easy, the
burden light? If not, how might this promise truly be fulfilled
in our daily lives?

Several things come to mind ....

We have all seen pictures of women carrying very heavy
burdens on their heads. They can do this only when they walk
in perfect balance. When their balance is right, the weight of
the load feels significantly reduced. How is the balance in your
life – between work, rest and play, between your relationship
with God and your relationship with God's world?

The gospel speaks of a yoke, and a yoke is usually the piece
of equipment that joins two creatures together so that they
are able to draw a heavy load in unison. Jesus invites us to be
yoked to him as we plough the furrows of our lives. It's not all
down to us, and this is a deeply liberating truth.

And finally, the effort required to carry out the tasks that
come our way depends very much on how much we desire

to do them. There is a huge difference between doing the weekly supermarket shop, and shopping to choose a gift for someone you love. When our desire is engaged the burden will seem light. It's like the difference between swimming with the current or against it.

One more thing: how many of us have set out on a hike with a backpack full of things we probably didn't need? How is your spiritual backpack? What are you carrying with you on this journey? Are there any old resentments or unfinished business that could be resolved by reaching out to someone from whom you are estranged? Are there any apologies due or gestures of reconciliation to be offered? Don't walk on with a backpack full of stones. Leave them behind, to make the space for grace.

As you reflect back over this first full week of our journey do any invitations you feel you have received come to mind, and what is encouraging you to travel further? The following questions may provide a few prompts as you reflect. Use anything that is helpful and leave aside all that is not. Stay with, and ponder, anything that particularly captures your imagination and attention.

Do you have any memories of heightened moments or experiences that you would call 'burning bushes'? Keep on going back to them. They are God-given fuel for your journey.

How do you feel about the encounter between the pregnant Elizabeth and the pregnant Mary? Have you ever had a moment of recognition, or resonance, with another person when you felt your souls were connecting?

Would you find it helpful to have an ongoing relationship with a spiritual companion?

The invitation to 'prepare a way for the Lord' isn't a demand to construct a motorway, but a call to walk the path of our own lives in such a way that it becomes a reflection of the Way of the gospel. How might you respond to this invitation in practice?

When Elisha receives the cloak of prophecy from Elijah he is already part of a long continuum of those who have faithfully ploughed life's furrow. Now he is receiving a commission to communicate the divine message in new ways to those who will follow after. To what extent can you identify with him?

What does the call to put out into deep water mean to you? Do you sense any impulse to go deeper, and can you risk the loss of control involved in going out of your depth?

Can you believe that your own life has its own true note that is destined to take its place in the great symphony of creation? What makes your instrument come to life and *sing*?

During this week you have been offered six very different invitations to engage with your soul's journey. Which of them most speaks to your heart?

Next week we will move on to consider a few signposts along the way that might help us develop a sense of direction.

SECOND WEEK OF LENT

Signposts

MONDAY
One step at a time

Your word is a lamp for my feet, and a light for my path.
(Psalm 119:105)

A young man of 32, a theologian and (then) Anglican priest, made a trip, many years ago, to the Mediterranean. As trips go it wasn't a resounding success. First of all, our traveller became very ill with a fever that nearly killed him. While in the recovery phase he was struck down by severe homesickness. He took a boat back for part of the journey, only to find himself and the boat becalmed and going nowhere. This run of bad luck might have put him off travel for a very long time. In fact, it inspired one of our most familiar hymns:

> *Lead kindly light amid the encircling gloom, lead thou me on.*
> *The night is dark and I am far from home, lead thou me on.*
> *Keep thou my feet, I do not ask to see*
> *The distant scene, one step enough for me.*
> John Henry Newman

The truth of his insight came home to me during a much more enjoyable, and much shorter journey. It was a dark November night in a remote Cumbrian village high in the hills. There was no street lighting, and only a faint glow of starlight provided a very tenuous clue to the course of the path we were walking to get to the village pub a mere kilometre away, for the annual bonfire and fireworks display.

I had at least had the foresight to bring a torch with

me, and I held it straight out, horizontally, in front of me, optimistically assuming that it would illuminate the way ahead beyond all stumbling. I was wrong. The pathetic little beam from the torch simply dissolved into the 'encircling gloom'. The surrounding darkness seemed to be laughing at me.

There was, of course, an obvious solution, one that Newman understood two centuries ago. When I lowered the torch and focused its beam on the path just ahead of me, its light became useful. I could now clearly see the ground beneath my feet, and, by taking one careful step after another, I arrived at the pub. Newman wouldn't have been impressed by this little odyssey but it was a lesson for me, one I have tried to apply in my everyday life.

The first signpost on our journey this week might well be this: to trust that all we need is light on the next step, and not a complete map of the way ahead. We know this in theory, but in practice there is always a nagging desire to know much more than we really need to know. We don't feel in control of our journey if all we can see is the next step. In practice we have no idea what lies around the next corner. What's more, if we focus on the 'distant scene', we may well fall over the boulders just in front of us. To be able to see the crucial 'one step' is not only all we need, but the only way to proceed with safety and confidence.

At a graduation ceremony the dean was giving out the degree certificates and asking new graduates what they were planning to do next. Some had great plans, for stellar careers in various professions. They had it all mapped out. One, however, hesitated for a moment as she considered her immediate journey from the dais back to her seat, and said simply: 'I'm going to walk very carefully down these three steps.' How would I have answered that question? Am I so concerned with my plans for the next decade that I risk stumbling over the steps I'll take today?

In Kingston, Ontario in Canada, there is very straight path laid along the shore of Lake Ontario, that the local people call *The Philosophers' Walk*, because, they claim, these far-seeing sages needed to have a straight path to walk, with no risky curves and turns, lest in their ponderings on the meaning of life they might forget where to put their feet and fall into the lake.

Today's signpost assures us that God's *word is* a lamp for our feet and a light on our path. It can only be that if we become familiar with it. Once we learn to focus on the next step, rather than trying to second-guess the distant scene, we may find an inexhaustible gold-mine of wisdom and guidance in these ancient texts. There are many ways to enter into scripture in search of this kind of enlightenment. The practice of *lectio divina* has been mentioned. Another possibility is to meditate on an incident in scripture using our imagination, letting the details of the scene take shape in our minds, and entering into the scene as if we were there. There is a short guide to both of these techniques at the end of this book.

These *words* that are a lamp to our feet take me back to the purpose of our torchlight walk to the pub that night. The fireworks that we watched with great delight are a bit like these words. As you hold them in your hand you have no idea what potential is contained inside them, but then you light the touchpaper and these harmless-looking little packages rise to the skies and scatter light and colour across the dark night. We light the touchpaper on God's word when we give it our focused attention, honestly seeking to discover its potential to enlighten our darkness and guide our ways.

Pause ...

... to ask for the grace to trust that the light that is given for our next few steps is all we need.

TUESDAY
Stay connected

Remain in me, and I in you. As a branch cannot bear
fruit by itself, unless it remains part of the vine,
neither can you unless you remain in me.
I am the vine, you are the branches. Whoever remains in me,
and I in that person, bears fruit in plenty;
for apart from me you can do nothing.
(John 15:4-5)

The metaphor of the vine and the grapes is very organic, like so many of Jesus' parables. He obviously drew deeply on the wisdom of the natural world, and this was echoed once for me during a day of reflection. We had been invited to share something of our own experience of finding God in the world around us. One participant told us that she worked as an assistant in a greengrocer's shop. She was at work all day and when she got home she had a family of teenagers to feed and a house to run, and, she admitted, that left very little time for prayer.

However, she said, whenever she had a few minutes' respite in the shop she would just focus her attention on the display of grapes. This always took her back to Jesus' self-description as 'the true vine', and she contemplated herself as a grape on that vine, along with every other grape whatever its size or colour or degree of sweetness. Every time she did this, she discovered fresh ways of understanding her relationship with the true vine, but she hadn't ever thought of this as prayer. In fact, it was pure contemplation and all of us who heard her were deeply moved.

There is no hierarchy, no sense of dominance or control in the metaphor of the vine. Everything is part of a greater wholeness, each with its own role, from the root to the branches to the fruits. Each element contributes in its own way to the fruitfulness, but this is only possible if the whole vine remains connected. If the grapes were to decide to leave the vine, they would not survive. The vine itself would survive, but it would be diminished. This might give us pause for thought in these times of social and political fragmentation.

The parable of the vine is a powerful call to build and sustain community. To insist on our total autonomy, either as individuals or as nations, is to court disaster. If we achieve what we say we desire, we will wither on the vine. The energy of life flows through the whole vine and without it the grapes cannot live. The logic is obvious, but how to live the truth of it is less clear. How do we nourish the bonds that connect us without turning them into shackles?

I was walking one day in a little copse when I noticed a dead leaf apparently dancing in the air. It seemed to be unattached to any branch, and I wondered idly why it didn't either fly away or fall to the ground. An hour later I returned to the same spot and to my amazement the same leaf was still there, dancing in the air. When I came closer to investigate, I could see a very fine, infinitely delicate but immensely strong thread, probably spun by a tiny tenacious spider, almost invisible to the naked eye, that connected the leaf to a nearby branch.

If the leaf had not been connected, it would indeed have flown away or dropped to the ground. But what if that connection, instead of being a fine, flexible filament, had been a rigid steel bar? The leaf would have been connected, but it would not have danced. This led me to wonder about the bonds in my own life, that link me to others, and to God.

The connection of the grape to the vine is a model of how connection should be. The vine holds the grape firmly and provides its nourishment and means of growth, but it also leaves it free to become the unique grape it has the potential to be. We are connected to the true vine by a thread so strong that it can never be broken, and so gentle that it will always leave us free to dance.

Soon afterwards I met someone who had been an accomplished liturgical dancer until a new priest had forbidden her to dance in 'his' church. For six years she had been obedient to this injunction. When she heard the story of the dancing leaf, she got to her feet, and she danced – the most beautiful liturgical dance. She had re-discovered her freedom in the power of the vine.

You might like to use Jesus' words for lectio divina: *Remain in me, and I in you.*

Pause ...

... to ask for the grace to remain always consciously connected to the source of our being and to rejoice in the freedom this connection offers us.

WEDNESDAY
Drink from your own well

Drink the water from your own storage well,
fresh water from your own spring.
(Proverbs 5:15)

Wells figure quite frequently in scripture, and in much indigenous spirituality wells are regarded as sacred space – places where the divine energy is especially evident. This is hardly surprising, since wells are a source of pure water, and water is essential to life. In Derbyshire, England, close to where I live, there is a tradition of annual well-dressing, when local wells are decorated with tableaux formed of flowers and other natural material to depict scenes from scripture. This is done to celebrate the importance of the well and its pure water and the fact that in the past these villages had been spared the plague.

Long before there was running water on tap in our households, there were wells. The needful water had to be fetched from a very local source, often at the heart of the village. No wonder the writer of Proverbs urges us to draw water from our own well. What would have been obvious to the people of the time is something far removed from our own experience. We expect water to be provided from somewhere else, somewhere remote, with some 'water authority' responsible for maintaining the supply. Do we make the same assumption about the source of our spiritual guidance and wisdom? Do we expect it to be provided by an external authority?

Today's scripture urges us to 'drink from our own well'

and not rely on second-hand wisdom delivered by others, who may or may not be trustworthy. So what does this mean in practice?

When I was drafting my first book, Landmarks, we had a young theology student staying with us. When he asked to see the draft I apologised for my lack of any theological background. His reply surprised me. 'The first line of theology is our own experience,' he said. 'Everything else represents a level of indirection.' This isn't to suggest that we don't need any formal academic theologians, but that, for most of us, theology, or the observation of the action of the living God, will be in the depth of our own experience, our own well.

There is a very useful bucket available to draw water from this well. It is another approach to prayer that has been used through the centuries by generations of spiritual pilgrims, and is variously called the Examen, or the Review of the Day prayer. This takes the form of a short time of looking back over the day, or the past few days, noticing what has happened, how we responded, and how we felt about it, what has drawn us closer to God and to each other and what, if anything has tended to pull us away from that true centre. A brief guide to this form of prayer is provided at the end of this book. Whatever particular form this takes for you, it is clear that it is centred on the well within us, where we believe God is indwelling.

A well from which to draw our daily water is essential if we are on a journey, because it is always with us. I remember, with some embarrassment, our daughter's first school nativity play. Because she had blonde hair and a cherubic expression, the teacher chose her to be an angel. This left me, her incompetent mother, with the challenge of creating an angel outfit, and my dismay must have been obvious, given that I can hardly sew a button on straight. She reported the problem to her teacher and the next day came home with the reassuring message: 'Never mind, if all else fails, you can always be a camel.' (Apparently there were camel outfits in the school store cupboard.) This event took its place in the family annals, and when she later had to sit exams or attend interviews, we would remind her that 'if all else fails you can always be a camel'.

We may smile, but when you are on a journey through the desert, in daily need of water but far from any supply, there are worse things to be than a camel. A camel carries its water within it, just as we carry our deepest source of wisdom and guidance within us, where the Holy Spirit is at home and where our unique personal experience of God and of the world is being constantly processed. The habit of looking back regularly over our lived experience is the basis of the art of reflective living. When we reflect on our experience in the light of grace and under the guidance of God, that experience turns into wisdom, which in turn shapes and forms the way we live in the future. It is the sacred alchemy that transforms the iron of ordinary daily events into the gold of a deeper relationship with God and with each other.

Today's signpost points back into our own hearts and our own lived experience. It invites us to make friends with our inner camel.

Pause ...

... to ask for the grace to trust that the deepest heart-wisdom the Holy Spirit desires to reveal to us is to be found in our own daily lived experience.

THURSDAY

Bag drop

Jesus looked hard at the rich young man and loved
him and said, 'You are lacking in one thing: go and sell
whatever you own and give the money to the poor, and
you will have treasure in heaven; then come, follow me.'
But at this saying he baulked and he went away grieving,
for he had many possessions.
(Mark 10:21-22)

There's a programme currently on TV in Britain, called *Rich Kids Go Skint*. It's about very privileged young people spending a few days with a family living on social security benefits, and struggling to put food on the table. Most episodes begin by showing the 'rich kid' in his or her usual habitat, enjoying a level of jaw-dropping affluence, and the 'poor family' in their daily struggle to keep going. Often the rich kid has a low opinion in general of those who struggle, assuming that it is somehow down to their lack of effort, and the poor family rather despises, in general, those who in their view enjoy obscene wealth. Invariably, by the end of each episode, when they have spent time getting to know and understand each other in a personal way, these attitudes have changed dramatically. The rich young man in the Bible might well have been a candidate for this programme.

On the face of it, the gospel story of the rich young man is disconcerting, to say the least, leaving most of us who have enough to live on and maybe a bit more (enough money, for example, to buy a book, and enough leisure to read it) feeling rather uncomfortable. I'm reminded of the saying: 'Jesus comes to comfort the afflicted and to afflict the comfortable'. And yet the account of the conversation between Jesus and the young man is clearly conducted in a spirit of real love and compassion on Jesus' part. How are we to receive and respond to the requirement to 'Sell everything, give to the poor and follow me'?

It reminds me of that point at the airport, when you have checked in for your flight and are about to go through security – the bag drop. This moment, for me, is a point of real relief. I no longer have to drag my 20kgs round the airport. I'm no longer responsible for that bag. Someone else will get it to the destination. Now I can focus on the journey ahead, free of most encumbrances. Yet our rich young man felt no such relief, only sadness, because he had a great many encumbrances. The difference between him and me, the reason why he felt sadness and I feel relief, is that he knew that this would be a last goodbye to his possessions, whereas I know that all 20kgs of them will be waiting for me to collect again from the baggage carousel at my destination.

Today's signpost points to a very radical 'bag drop'. We are not necessarily, or even usually, being asked literally to sell off our homes and live on the streets, but to consider the extent of the encumbrances that dominate our consciousness and prevent us from living the deep demands of the gospel. The very disturbing underlying question is this: 'How important is my own comfort, security and wellbeing compared to the comfort, security and wellbeing of others, my neighbours, and those in other lands?' If we are honest, and because we are programmed for survival, inevitably we will realise that our own wellbeing, and that of those we love, rates a lot more highly than the wellbeing of others, and if push comes to shove we will fight our own corner before we will fight theirs. This is how individuals think and behave. This is how nations think and behave.

Is Jesus really suggesting that we can overcome this instinct and move from egotism to altruism – just like that? Let's go back to the story, and notice that Jesus looks upon us, as he looked upon the rich young man, with love. The young man, for his part, is grieving, but it doesn't quite feel like the end of the story. Maybe in time, given infinite patience on Jesus' part, he will gradually be able to let go of all that is holding him back.

We are facing very big questions like this in our own times and we too are feeling sadness, frustration, guilt and a whole range of emotions at our own inability to make the sacrifices that we increasingly see are going to be asked of us. What are we being asked to leave at the bag drop, and *not* pick up again a few hours later? Are we willing to step up our support of those in need, through financial aid, local food banks, volunteering and real empathy and companionship? Are we willing to reduce our travel by road, sea and air, to lessen the impact of our lifestyle on the planet? Are we open to working much more cooperatively in the family of nations, assisting those whose economies are struggling?

When we leave this earthly life we will take with us exactly the same amount of baggage with which we first arrived. Is it time to let go of the accumulations of the intervening years, and to focus more on the journey itself than on the 'stuff' we are carrying with us?

Pause ...

... to ask for the grace to let go of what we can spare, and then to let go of a little bit more than we can spare, learning to live simply, so that others may simply live.

FRIDAY
A lesson in love

'You have heard how it was said, "You shall love your neighbour and hate your enemy". But I say this to you, love your enemies and pray for those who persecute you.'
(Matthew 5:43-44)

This command, to love our neighbour as we love ourselves, and then to extend our love to those who do not mean well with us, is probably the best-known text in scripture, and is the basis of the Golden Rule that almost all human beings, of whatever race or creed regard as the foundation of what it means to be the best we can be. It is the best known, the most quoted, and also the hardest of all scriptural commands to live by.

Why is it so hard to love our neighbour? Why do most of us not really even love (or at least *like)* ourselves? And as for loving our enemies, well, forget it. Just an idealistic dream, we might think. Whatever we do to try to force ourselves to feel love for another, unless it comes naturally, it just doesn't seem to work. Is it just a command to which we are only, at best, able to pay lip service? Yet if we are on a journey towards the best we can be as human beings, then surely such a strong and central directive can't be ignored.

The breakthrough for me came in a comment by M. Scott Peck, who asserts that love, in this context, is not an emotion but a decision. The clouds of confusion disappeared, and suddenly I could see how it might be possible to view the problem of love very differently.

Of course love is an emotion, as we all know. Of course love is something we feel. But if M. Scott Peck is right, it is also something much more than this, something much less subjective, something we could really attempt to put into practice. Because decisions are in our power. Emotions are not.

Once I began to reflect on the implications of this insight, the nature of Jesus' command became much clearer. It's not, I realised, a question of trying to force the way we *feel*, but a call to make our *choices* in the light of what love asks of us – or, put another way, what the best in us would choose. This is a very tough call, but it's not impossible. It lies at the very heart of what it will mean to evolve spiritually towards the best we can be – the human being fully live, and fully reflecting the glory of God. So how do we do it?

Let's start with ourselves. Loving ourselves isn't a licence to indulge, but a reminder that we need to be kind to ourselves. We may not always like what we see when we look in the mirror, but we can *choose* to care for ourselves, for example by eating a healthy diet, getting enough rest and exercise and attending to our friendship circles. Because if we don't have any care for ourselves, we have little chance of authentically caring for our neighbour.

And then the neighbour… Perhaps you live next door to the neighbour from hell. Maybe he complains every time the dog barks or a branch from your tree overhangs into his garden. But imagine this scenario. He's alone, with no friends or family. He suffers a heart attack. He's going to be at home, and out of action for a long time. How is he going to get to the shops? You have a choice. You can leave him to work things out as best he can. Or you can go round, risk his bad temper, and offer to help. What does love ask of you?

We might manage to apply this practice with friends, and even with difficult neighbours, but enemies? In 1944 a parade of captured German soldiers was force-marched through Red Square in Moscow. A furious throng of Muscovites had assembled. The Russian people had suffered devastating losses at the hands of the regime these prisoners represented, so cordons had been set up to prevent the people from physically attacking them. The prisoners filed past. The officers still held their heads high and were jeered and spat upon by the crowd. Then came the ordinary soldiers, wounded, starving, exhausted, terrified. A complete silence descended. Then one woman looked into the eyes of one prisoner and saw not an enemy but a starving human being. She slipped back to her home and returned with a crust of bread. She broke through the cordon and gave the bread to the first prisoner she encountered. When other people saw this they began to do the same, breaking through the barriers to give some morsel of food to these starving men.

They didn't *feel* *l*ove for these soldiers, some of whom may have killed their loved ones, but they made a decision to do the most loving thing they could do in the circumstances. They demonstrated that it is actually possible to 'love your enemy'.

Pause ...

... to ask for the grace to respond to both friend and enemy in the light of the question: What is love asking of me in this situation; what is the more loving thing to do next?

SATURDAY
Choose life

I am offering you life or death, blessing or curse.
Choose life, then, so that you and your descendants
may live in the love of the Lord your God.
(Deuteronomy 30:19)

My small granddaughter is more excited than usual as she rushes to show me a corner of their drive, where she has found a perfect little clump of wild pansies pushing their way, with dogged determination, through the tarmac. She squeals with delight.

In a sleepy cul-de-sac in the suburbs two new parents are settling into their home again after three months alongside their very premature baby girl in intensive care. The long days while she was fighting for her life are behind them. Life with all its promise lies ahead for her now like an open road. They open a greeting card from a neighbour. It reads: 'She believed she could do it, and she did it.' Their hearts leap. Life has triumphed.

A middle-aged hiker makes it to the summit of the mountain on her prosthetic leg. It's a sponsored walk for her favourite charity and there was no way she wasn't going to take part. Her friends surround her as they reach their destination, and give her a big congratulatory hug.

All around us we see and hear stories like these. Life, it seems, is really on our side, nourishing us, encouraging us, helping us to achieve what we thought was impossible. But does it work both ways? Are *we* always on the side of life?

Today we reach a crucial crossroads in our journey, one

that we will encounter again and again along the way, and there is a clear signpost, calling us, in everything we do to 'choose life'. What does this mean and how do we do it?

On the face of it the choice seems obvious. Who would not choose life over death, blessing over curse? But of course it's not so simple, because blessings often come in disguise and things that appear to be life-enhancing can turn out to be death-dealing. And it's not so simple because most of us have a tendency to focus our attention more on what is going wrong than on what is flourishing.

I discovered this to my cost once in a period of meditation. I was reflecting on what I might call the 'field' of my life and I spent the best part of the morning mulling over all the things that had gone wrong: the things I had started enthusiastically but never carried through; the good ideas I had had that became choked up and killed off by complications; the overtures of friendship that had been undermined by someone's spiteful remarks or had landed on unreceptive ground and received no response. I could visualise all these things, and when the time of prayer was over I can also remember visualising a small patch of wheat that was growing and ripening in the sun, and then, in my imagination, walking straight past it, paying it no attention. Only at that point did the Holy Spirit intervene with an unforgettable reminder: 'Stop watering the weeds.'

We choose life when we give our energy and attention to what is life-giving, for ourselves and for others, just as we nourish and water the plants we want to grow. We only have a limited amount of energy. How often do we waste it on the 'weeds', the very things we do not want to grow.

It might be good to pause at this signpost and check out where you are currently focusing most of your energy and attention. Is it an issue that is helping to add to the store of love, trust and hope in yourself and the world, or is it something that is draining you, and the world, of energy? Would you call it a 'plant' or a 'weed'?

What we feed, with our energy and attention, will grow. What we starve, by withholding or withdrawing our energy, will shrivel and die. What aspects of our lives and our world do we want to grow? We choose life every time we give our energy and attention to those things that nourish life for all. And when we do so, we can be assured that life itself will be empowering, helping and supporting us in every way.

Pause ...

... to ask for the grace to focus our energy and attention where it is most likely to nourish the spirit of life.

SABBATH PAUSE
The way forward

You have already been told what is good
And what the LORD seeks from you:
Only this, to do what is right,
To love loyalty and to walk humbly with your God.
(Micah 6:8)

During this past week we have explored a few signposts along the path. Time now for a sabbath pause, as we rest at this final signpost of the week and reflect on the wisdom it gives us for the way ahead. You might like to begin your sabbath time by pondering these words from the prophet Micah. Just sit with them, and let them soak into your mind and heart and notice anything that strikes you – especially anything that resonates with your actual lived experience.

Micah suggests three simple hallmarks of an authentic journey to the best we can become: right action, love and humility.

In his earthly ministry Jesus was very emphatic about the importance of *orthopraxis* (right action) and apparently much less concerned about *orthodoxy* (right belief). It's rather ironic that much traditional religious practice reverses this emphasis, so that the demands of orthodoxy can become dominant.

Justice is a prime requirement of 'right action' or 'right living' and is a direct consequence of living by the demands of love. When we reflected on what we might need to leave at the Bag Drop, we came up against the uncomfortable fact that much of our own comfort and wellbeing is maintained at the expense of others in our world, and at the expense of Earth herself and all her creatures.

To love loyalty is a big ask, even in our relationships with those close to us. The chances of any love towards those who would harm us seem non-existent, yet events in Red Square in 1944 tell a different story. What happens if we forget the pink ribbons and St Valentine's hearts and think, instead, of love as a decision. We can do nothing to change our feelings, but we can do everything to shape our choices. 'What love asks of us' is never going to be an easy question to face. It's not a theoretical proposition that we can contemplate at our leisure. It's a moment by moment challenge that urges us to ask, 'In the situation in which I find myself right now, what is the more loving thing to do next?'

This will rarely provide a black and white answer. Sometimes it may even require a choice of the least of the evils. It will never be easy, but we are invited to make choices in such a way that our dominant attitude to life will be love, compassion and gratitude. The Review prayer gives us a very helpful way of checking out the actual choices we are making on a daily basis and whether they are drawing us closer to the best we can be or tending to pull us further away from our best. We make our journey one step at a time, one choice at a time, and the raw material for that journey is discovered in our own experience, our own well.

Humility is the art of not assuming that our way is the best or the only way. It enables us to see the situation as it really is, and not through the lens of 'how does this affect me?'. It shrinks our ego and opens our mind and heart to embrace all that is 'other'. It enables us to speak truth to power with integrity and not merely from our own need to assert ourselves. Paradoxically, humility turns out to be far more powerful than human power, because it springs from the power of the Holy Spirit. Human power exerts power *over* others, often abusively, in order to boost itself. The power of the holy Spirit works the other way round. It *empowers* us from within.

Jesus describes himself as 'the Way'. He invites us to follow him if we want to know the way. First, we follow him through his earthly ministry, learning from him 'on the job' as he shows us what it looks like in a human life to respond to the demands of justice and love. And then he invites us to follow him through a dark valley, where we discover the cost of living true to the best we can be. He urges us not to be afraid when we face the opposition that the true life will inevitably provoke, the shadow that the light will reveal. 'Stay with me,' he urges us, 'and don't be afraid, because I am walking every step with you, and together we will transcend the worst that the darkness can inflict.' Life itself is a Lenten journey, sometimes hard, with stony stretches, but it leads to the fullness of a life beyond our comprehension, that we might call Easter.

Jesus' repeated invitation is disarmingly simple: *Follow me.* He doesn't say 'Worship me'. He doesn't say 'Go to church'. He says *Follow me.* And this means quite simply learning to track his footsteps and walk the way he models. The way may get steeper next week as we encounter a few obstacles.

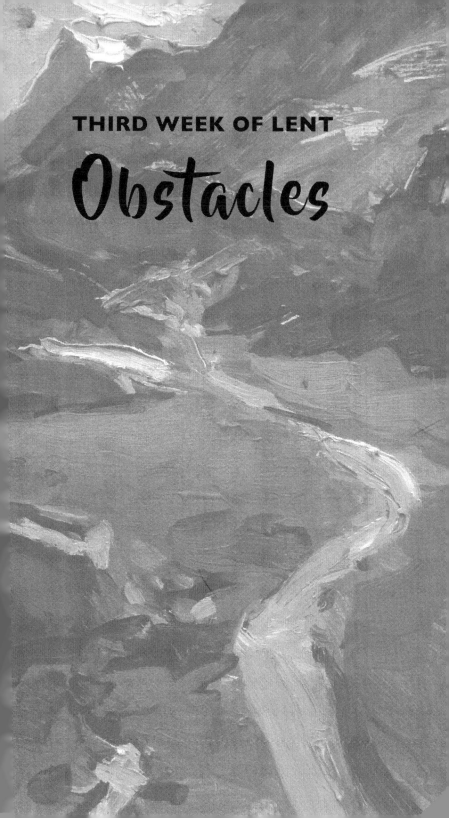

THIRD WEEK OF LENT

Obstacles

MONDAY

Judgement

'Do not judge and you will not be judged;
because the judgements you give are the judgements
you will get, and the standard you use will be the standard
used for you. Why do you observe the splinter in your brother's
eye and never notice the log in your own?'
(Matthew 7:1-3)

If I stopped to count the number of times I pass judgements every day, either in explicit comments or, more frequently, in the cold silence of a hardened heart, I would have to admit that this warning is for me.

Take for example, that day at work, when a colleague and I were standing at the window of our seventh-floor office in one of the more derelict areas of a northern English city.

As we watched, we noticed someone waiting beside the main entrance at street level. It was apparent that he had mobility problems and was building up the confidence to tackle the revolving door. As he stood there, hesitant and apprehensive, another man left the building through the same revolving door, and with what seemed like a shocking lack of consideration, brushed past the waiting man, almost knocking him over in his haste. With a brusque 'Sorry', thrown back over his shoulder to the person he had almost toppled, he sped off.

'Did you see that?' I asked my colleague. 'What a brute – he almost knocked that person over, and barely managed a curt apology.'

My colleague was quiet for a moment, before responding:

'Yes, it looked really bad,' he agreed, 'but I know that man who came rushing out. He's blind.'

I was stunned into silence, and Jesus' warning rang out loud in my mind. The second man's blindness cast a wholly different light on the matter. He never even saw the man he so nearly caused to tumble. If I had known that, I would never have been so judgemental. His apparent rudeness was a mere splinter, easy to excuse if you simply knew the facts. My judgement, however, was a huge log, making me far more blind, inwardly, than the person I was so ready to condemn. The problem with having a huge log in your eye is that you can't even see the log, let alone anyone else's splinters. My own huge log, that day, was my own subconscious assumption that there was nothing at all wrong with my eyesight.

The first challenge is to know ourselves, and our very real limitations. This is a first step, at least, to acknowledging that everyone else also has their limitations, and their outward appearance or behaviour may not reflect the person inside, who may be struggling with all kinds of issues quite invisible to the casual observer. How easy it is to notice and to judge another person's wounding words or conduct. How difficult to perceive the woundedness within that person that gives rise to it. That depth of vision is not in our gift. It is the mark of divine vision. It follows that only God can ever wholly know the circumstances that shape our words and actions, and only that depth of knowledge can give rise to true understanding.

Perhaps alarm bells are ringing as we read that the standard by which we judge each other will be the standard by which we ourselves will be judged. I still reproach myself for my readiness that day to condemn another person without having any knowledge of that person's own needs and limitations. The standard I so short-sightedly applied to him I now must apply to myself. This isn't about some distant court in heaven, but about the action of the Holy Spirit probing our hearts in the here and now.

Whenever we raise our hand to point a finger at another

person, three other fingers are pointing back towards ourselves. While we may find plenty to criticise in other people, the only person we have any real chance of changing is ourself.

Pause ...

... to ask for the grace to leave all judgement to God, who alone knows the heart of the matter.

TUESDAY

Prejudice

Philip found Nathanael and said to him,
'We have found him of whom Moses in the Law and the
prophets wrote, Jesus son of Joseph, from Nazareth.
Nathanael said to him, 'From Nazareth? Can anything good
come from Nazareth?' Philip replied, 'Come and see.'
When Jesus saw Nathanael coming towards him he said of him,
'Here, truly, is an Israelite in whom there is no deception.'
(John 1:45-47)

Nathanael's encounter with Jesus offers a delightful vignette along our journey, but there is a sting in the tail. Nathanael is sitting under the fig tree, minding his own business. Philip runs up, bursting with excitement, to announce that he has met the Messiah. I wonder how I would react to such a claim. I can already feel the cynicism rising up. Yeah right! It gets worse when Philip reveals that the Messiah comes from Nazareth. Imagine someone telling you that the Messiah has arrived and was born and raised in a not very well-regarded town near you. No way! Nathanael is seeing everything through the lens of his own assumptions and prejudices.

But let's see where Jesus stands on this interaction. Having only just seen Nathanael sitting under the fig tree, Jesus says: This is a true son of Israel. This guy is the real deal. There is no deceit in him. He is seeing Nathanael through the lens of God's viewfinder.

This story carries warnings of two big obstacles lying in our path towards the best we can be. The first is our attitude to the 'other' in our midst. The second is our difficulty in recognising and empowering that which is 'without deceit' in times when lies and deceit are the hallmarks of the very systems that govern us.

In our world today, and shockingly in our own country, there is a problem with our attitude to 'the other'. It's part of the human condition to be distrustful of what we don't know or understand. Maybe we needed such caution when we were living from hand to mouth on the savannah, but now such distrust can seriously undermine our human communities and impede our spiritual growth.

Nathanael at first sees Jesus as we perhaps see others who are not 'our kind of people'. They may look different in obvious ways – different ethnicity, different kinds of clothing, or they may sound different, speak with an unfamiliar accent, or have a grating voice. Or they may have chosen a lifestyle that is alien to our own way of seeing things – different religious beliefs or practice, different political views, different ways of forming personal relationships. These attitudes can distort our inter-personal relationships, and also lead us to take action as a nation that we would never contemplate taking personally – colluding with collective decisions that marginalise our neighbours while remaining blind to the huge deceptions with which we are being systematically indoctrinated.

What might help us to see the true colours of those we meet? One way is to practise the habit of seeking to notice 'that of God' in everyone we meet. It helps also to bear in mind that everything and everyone is still a work in progress. When a caterpillar is about to become a butterfly there is a magical moment, just as the chrysalis is getting ready to release the freshly transformed butterfly, when the outer skin of the chrysalis becomes transparent and the true colours of the new creature show through. We sometimes glimpse these moments in each other – and in strangers – when we feel, as Jesus recognised in Nathanael, that we are seeing the true heart of the other person, perhaps reflected in their eyes, perhaps expressed in their words or actions.

What guidance does this incident give us as we struggle

with the growing tendencies in our own society towards nationalism, protectionism and xenophobia and other forms of collective intolerance? How might we work against these dangerous tendencies?

What is helping us to recognise the best in each other, and helping us to grow beyond our fear and distrust of 'the other' in our midst?

What do you feel is reinforcing our prejudices? If national policies are jarring against your own true convictions which way will you go? How far will you collude? How might you resist what you know in your heart is rooted in deception?

Have you had any interaction recently with someone with a different outlook from your own? How did that feel? Have you learned anything from it? Has anything surprised you? Has anything challenged your assumptions or expectations?

I have friends in Australia who run a little retreat house called *Nathanael's Rest*, a name they sometimes abbreviate to *Nat's Rest*. Their son, who has a wicked sense of humour, likes to transpose this into *Rats' Nest*.

When we look around us, or tune into the daily news and see some of our politicians deliberately deceiving us in their own pursuit of power and ambition, we might justifiably feel we are living in a rats' nest. How might we use our energy to help transform our country, our society and ourselves into a true reflection of who we are called to be, people in whom there is no deceit?

Pause ...

... to ask for the grace to 'sit under the fig tree' and reflect on what kind of 'Nazareth' we believe can never yield anything good. And while we are there, to let Jesus look upon us, and affirm the truth he sees in *our* heart.

WEDNESDAY
The blame chain

God said (to Adam) 'Who told you that you were naked?
Have you been eating from the tree from which I forbade
you to eat?' The man replied, 'The woman you gave to be
with me, she gave me fruit from the tree, and I ate it.'
Then the Lord God said to the woman, 'What is this
that you have done?' The woman replied,
'The snake tempted me and I ate.'
(Genesis 3:11-13)

It seems to be a characteristic of human nature that whenever something goes wrong we look for someone else to blame for it. It begins in the schoolyard, with the perpetual childhood cry of 'It wasn't me!' And it rises to the boardroom and the cabinet office. It begins in Genesis and rolls right down through the millennia, to block our own journey. Because this is a *chain* – the blame chain, and this chain has serious consequences. It perpetuates injustice by scapegoating innocent people, and it prevents us from acknowledging and learning from our own mistakes.

We see the same reaction in the highest echelons of power. If our leaders can't get the outcome they desire, it's the fault of other countries who are being deliberately obstructive. If the economy is in trouble it's the fault of the other political party who left us with all their problems (even if that party hasn't held office for decades.) And worst of all, if things are not going well, it's the fault of the immigrants, the foreigners, those with a different faith or a different lifestyle. The original sin of laying the blame for all that has gone wrong

85

with humanity at the door of poor Eve has been perpetuated, with terrible consequences, all down the ages, often covering up the naked truths of social, emotional, physical and sexual abuse.

What makes us erect the blame chain and get locked behind it? A big clue is in God's question, 'Who told you that you were naked?' Nakedness is very scary. There is nowhere to hide. We can't cover up our flaws with elegant clothes or paint over our moles and scars with expensive makeup. Exposure can feel terrifying. It's as though someone is pointing a camera at us, and the only way we can stop them registering our flaws is to re-direct their attention to someone else. This takes the spotlight off ourselves, and gives us time to put some clothes on.

We feel naked when our ego is challenged, when we feel belittled, or our honour is impugned, when our team loses, when we behave foolishly, or don't get our own way, or when our tribe is criticised. There are thousands of links in the blame chain. The ego is the most powerfully defended part of who we are. It's like a hard shell surrounding that vulnerable spark of our true self. The problem is that if we truly desire to become the person we are destined to be, something will have to break open that shell, to allow our true self to hatch.

The ego shell will never break open as long as we can find someone else to blame for whatever has gone wrong. The blame chain fortifies our defences. It also stops our soul from hatching and prevents us from growing into the best we can be. This isn't just true for us as individuals. It applies equally to our nations. A nation that can only put itself first, at the expense of the greater good of humanity, is a nation solidly trapped in the ego-shell. A nation whose ego-shell has been shattered, perhaps by defeat or humiliation, is the nation that will learn from its mistakes, face its own history and continue its journey to the best it can be.

If you come up against the blame chain in your soul journey maybe you will find it helpful to ask yourself these questions:

- What nakedness in yourself are you trying to cover up, or divert attention from?
- Who are you trying to blame for the situation and how might this affect your chosen scapegoat?
- What opportunity for growth are you missing along your own journey by staying resolutely behind your blame chain?
- Do you see similar defensive scapegoating going on in your family, your community, your nation? If so, is there anything you can do or say to counteract it?

The key that releases the blame chain from its padlock is the honest acknowledgement of our own mistakes and faults. Then this obstacle can become a learning opportunity and a God-given, if painful, invitation to grow.

Pause ...

... to ask for the grace to stop passing the buck, and to discover instead what gift of enlightenment and insight 'the buck' has for us if we will only risk taking hold of it.

THURSDAY
Use it or lose it

'You are the salt of the earth. But if salt loses its taste, what can make it salty again? It is no longer good for anything, and can only be thrown out to be trampled underfoot. You are the light of the world. A city built on a hilltop cannot be hidden. No one lights a lamp and puts it under a tub; they put it on the lamp-stand where it shines for everyone in the house. In the same way your light must shine for people, so that they may see your good works and give praise to your Father in heaven.'
(Matthew 5:13-16)

On the face of it these comparisons are about gifts, and it's not obvious how gifts become obstacles. Yet there are clear warnings here. Being the salt of the earth is a gift, and a description we sometimes apply to people who seem to have absorbed the best of a long life and radiate its fruits out to others. But Jesus warns us that salt can lose its flavour and then it becomes useless.

Similarly, the light that has to be on a lamp-stand and not pushed under the bed where no-one can see it, or see by it. Of course it wouldn't make any sense to do that. And yet when it comes to that inner light we all have, which is our own personal gifting, we very often do precisely that. Jesus was a shrewd observer of human nature. Why do we so often hide, or fail to use, our gifts, and how might this be an obstacle on our soul journey?

I once led a weekend retreat for a group of people who all knew each other very well. Because I knew this, I risked starting the retreat with an invitation to them to share with the group what they felt their own unique gifting was. As I fully expected, the result was a deafening silence, and I knew that in their position I too would have been silent. After a few minutes of what one might call 'creative discomfort', I changed the question and invited them to share what they felt each other's unique gifting was. Then there was no holding back. They enthusiastically named the many gifts that others possessed.

Why is it so easy to recognise the gifts in others and so hard to acknowledge our own? Is it natural reticence, as if we were claiming some kind of 'achievement'? If so, we are missing the meaning of the word *gift*. I was startled once by a Carmelite friar who came to the university chaplaincy to talk about the monastic life. Asked about the vow of poverty, he said: 'Poverty simply means we don't have money.' Shocked expressions all round. How does anyone manage without having any money? And then he added 'We only have the use of it.' While rather cynically thinking to myself that I could happily live without money if I just had the use of it, this comment really made me think. In fact, none of us really has anything. We only have the use of it. Of course we think we own our cars, our computers, our clothes. We bought them with our own money. And how did we earn the money? By using our *gifts*. Recognising that, ultimately, everything is gift, is very liberating, but it also brings responsibility. It matters how we use our gifts. It matters that we don't just pack them away in a cupboard, but *spend* them. It's not about possessing them. It's about having, and sharing, the use of them.

A South African woman, running an orphanage for children whose parents had died of AIDS, was asked, in an interview, what she hoped to leave behind as a legacy when her life was over. She replied: 'I hope that when I die I will stand before God with empty hands, because I have spent all the gifts I've been given. All I want to leave behind is a footprint showing someone else the way to this orphanage to continue caring for these children.'

Hoarding our gifts, and keeping them safe 'for a rainy day', is like putting our lamp under the bed. Unfortunately, it reflects a mindset that is all too common among Christians, who have been taught that the purpose of their faith journey is to be 'saved'. Personal salvation seems to dominate their faith, eclipsing the constant gospel call to allow themselves and their gifts to be spent, for the sake of the greater good of all creation. The result can be an insipid, defensive way of living and believing that has lost its spice and flavour and will never inspire anyone else to risk the soul journey. It is to risk losing the very thing we are so determined to save.

To be spent, however, to use our gifts creatively and for the greater good, is to bring the lamp out from under the bed, giving enlightenment not just for ourselves but for all creation.

Pause ...

... to ask for the grace to acknowledge and spend our gifts, and let no false reticence tempt us to consign them to eternal uselessness, under the bed.

FRIDAY
Settling for less

The Lord then said to Moses, 'Go down at once, for your people whom you brought up from the land of Egypt have gone wrong. They have been quick to leave the way that I ordered them to follow. They have cast themselves an image of a calf, worshipped it and offered sacrifice to it, shouting, "These are your gods, Israel, who brought you up from the land of Egypt!"'
(Exodus 32:7-8)

Once upon a time a traveller set out on a journey into the unknown, to seek his destiny. He travelled through many varied landscapes. Sometimes the path was smooth and easy and he had plenty of time to stop and smell the flowers. Sometimes the path became steep and stony and the sun beat down on him without mercy. Sometimes the clouds gathered and the gales blew and maybe he wished he had never set out.

But one sunny morning, to his great surprise, he caught sight of a figure coming towards him over the crest of the hill. The man was on horseback. Both horse and rider were decked in amazing livery. This was clearly a man who wielded power in the world.

The horseman stopped to talk to the traveller, and they shared something of their stories, their respective quests for their destiny. The traveller was envious of the horseman's wealth, and especially of his horse and all its trappings. Sensing the traveller's pangs of longing the horseman said: 'Tell you what …. If you can recite the Lord's Prayer for me, without any digressions or interruptions, I will give you the horse.'

Well, how difficult could that be? The traveller could hardly believe his ears. Of course I can do that. And he began. Line by line, phrase by phrase he thoughtfully and carefully recited the Lord's Prayer. He got as far as 'lead us not into temptation ...' and stopped, took a deep breath and said, 'Do I get the saddle as well?' And the horseman rode off into the sunset, and the traveller continued, on foot.

Once upon another time, another band of travellers set out on a journey to find their destiny. The children of Israel had left the place of captivity in Egypt to seek the place of promise in Canaan, led and guided by Moses, who was himself a man with a past and had become a man on a mission. Not just on a mission, but a man with a vision, because Moses communed directly with God. His charges gave him a hard time in very many ways. Leading them through the wilderness was a bit like herding cats. They very readily digressed into rebukes about the lack of water and the quality of the provisions. They were, in his own words, a wilful and wayward flock.

One day Moses had gone up the mountain for a private meeting with God. The people were getting restive, wondering why they didn't get to meet with God, and then they hit on the idea of making a god that they *could* access, without all the trouble of clambering up the mountain. And so they collected their gold rings and jewellery and melted them down to create a golden calf. They left the path that would lead them to their destiny in a place of freedom, and took a diversion into a track of their own making. They took what they thought was a short cut to God, by settling for a lifeless substitute.

An ancient tale from a faraway land in a very different culture? Or does this story hold up a mirror to our own tendency to be seduced away from what we know to be our soul's true course by our human tendency to settle for second best? We too lose patience in the long journey towards what we most truly long for. In our impatience we create lesser goals for ourselves – goals that will never satisfy our longings but merely offer fleeting pleasure when what we really seek is joy. We too become restive when life fails to deliver on what it seemed to promise, and we take our 'gold', in cash or on our credit cards, and turn it into something we can have and possess in the here and now, without the effort of climbing the mountain.

The goods we purchase with our golden calves will, not surprisingly, always leave us disappointed and disillusioned, but they have the power to mesmerise us and distract us from our true quest. They take many forms: the pursuit of status, wealth or power, the false consolation of casual sex or recreational drug use, or merely the trinkets continually on offer in a consumer culture. These golden calves are gilded obstacles along a journey that draws on our deeper strengths and guides us to a richer destiny.

We probably won't be asked to recite the Lord's Prayer without distraction, and we can only guess at how it felt when Moses kept disappearing into the mountain mists. But the diversions that derailed these ancient journeys are no less destructive in our own times.

Pause ...

... to ask for the grace to see beyond the lesser distractions that seduce us and to focus on the horizons of our true destiny

SATURDAY
Not my problem

'A man was on his way down from Jerusalem to Jericho and fell into the hands of bandits; they stripped him, beat him and then made off, leaving him half dead. Now by chance a priest was travelling down the same road, but when he saw the man, he passed by on the other side. In the same way a Levite who came to the place saw him, and passed by on the other side. But a Samaritan traveller who came on him was moved with compassion when he saw him.'
(Luke 10:30-34)

We all know the story of the Good Samaritan and how the representatives of 'the great and the good' walked by on the other side, leaving the victim to suffer alone, and how the Samaritan from the hated tribe was the one who not only stopped to help, but arranged, at his own expense, for the victim to be lovingly cared for.

Whatever excuses are found to exonerate the priest and the Levite, possibly afraid of staining their ritual purity or maybe genuinely lacking in compassion, the fact remains that it was the unlikely traveller, the much-maligned Samaritan, who demonstrated what it means to be 'a good neighbour'.

This familiar story found an echo in an incident related to me by a friend who herself had the misfortune to 'fall by the wayside' and who met her own version of the priest, the Levite and the Samaritan on a lonely trail on a rainy day on a remote Scottish island. This is the (true) story of her misadventure.

She was walking with a friend on the island of Iona, which lies off the island of Mull, which is itself accessible only by ferry from the west coast of mainland Scotland. It was raining, and the path was slippery. It also happened that at the time the island was host to more than the usual number of tourists, mainly from overseas, who were on a mission to follow up clues about the mysterious Holy Grail, suggested in the novel *The Da Vinci Code*

As they walked, she slipped on a wet patch of stone, fell and broke her ankle. Getting medical help on Iona involves the island nurse as the first responder, who then summons the doctor from Mull if necessary, who in turn can call for a helicopter rescue. The friend went for help from the nurse, and, of course, had to leave her injured companion sitting there, in pain and in the rain.

As she sat there a group of hikers approached, all intent on finding the Holy Grail clues. She greeted them and tried to warn them not to slip on the same stone that had caused her own downfall. Then she added: 'Are any of you by any chance doctors?'

The first man in the line looked down at her, thought for a moment and then announced: 'Well, we have a cardiologist, an anaesthetist and a paediatrician here. But sorry we don't have a doctor!' And with this startling and rather shocking disclosure he placed his hand on her shoulder to steady himself round the slippery patch, and they all walked on by.

All, that is, except for the last in the line, a woman, who sat down on the stone beside the casualty and said: 'I'm not a medic, and I don't have any first aid skills, but I'm not going to leave you here alone and in pain. I will sit here with you until help arrives.'

In the conversation that ensued between them, the woman revealed that she was from Philadelphia in the USA. The name *Philadelphia* derives from the Greek and means 'brotherly love'. It isn't hard to hear Jesus' question echoing down the ages to land on a rock on the island of Iona. 'Which of these do you think was the good neighbour to the person in need?'

Can we also hear the other part of Jesus' instruction: 'Go and do the same.' We might protest that in that situation we would also have tried to help, but the fact is that most of those present did not. Perhaps they were focused on the hunt for the Holy Grail. Perhaps they were focused on the small print on their medical indemnity insurance policies. And perhaps it was the woman from Philadelphia who found her own Holy Grail that wet morning on Iona when she responded to what love was asking of her.

The road to Jericho is everywhere today. Hour on hour people are being attacked, beaten and left for dead, either literally in a violent urban culture or global conflict, or by relentless sadistic bullying on social media, by punitive social systems that drive so many to crushing desperation in their losing battle to support themselves and their families, or by the ravages of physical, sexual or emotional exploitation in abusive relationships.

How easy it is to walk on by, because, after all, it's not really our problem. Is it?

Pause ...

... to ask for the grace to recognise our neighbour's need and respond to it with sisterly/brotherly love.

SABBATH PAUSE
Come on down

*Zacchaeus was a chief tax collector and a wealthy man.
He kept trying to see which Jesus was, but he was too short
and could not see him for the crowd; so he ran ahead and
climbed a sycamore tree to catch a glimpse of Jesus as
he was to pass that way. When Jesus reached the spot he
looked up and said to him, 'Zacchaeus, come down.
Hurry, for I am to stay at your house today.'
And he hurried down and welcomed him joyfully.*
(Luke 19:2-6)

I spent a large part of my childhood up a tree, so I have a
lot of fellow feeling with Zacchaeus. As an only child in a
neighbourhood with no other children nearby, my playground
was the wood at the bottom of my parents' garden, and my
favourite spot in that wood was a very specific tree with very
climbable branches. I used to perch up there and watch the
world go by. Not that very much of the world went by. It
was more a vantage point where I could 'collect my thoughts
and think them over'. Zacchaeus, by contrast, had a far more
interesting encounter, poised among the branches of his
sycamore tree.

And what better place to spend some quiet sabbath time
today than swathed in the foliage of a sycamore tree?

Zacchaeus' motive for his choice of grandstand seat was
quite simply that he was short, and therefore unlikely to catch
sight of Jesus among the crowds. But as the story proceeds,
we learn that something rather different was going to happen.
Jesus does indeed go home with Zacchaeus, and they have

quite a heart-to-heart conversation, during which Zacchaeus has to face a good deal about himself and the way he has conducted his life thus far. He climbs the tree hoping for sight of Jesus. He comes down from the tree to discover insight into himself.

Maybe this is a pattern we could recognise. Our human search for knowledge, status or achievement pushes us *up* the tree of ambition. The real prize, of self-knowledge, is only discovered when we come *down*, recognise our limitations, and become open to the potential of grace flowing from a deeper source.

This week's journey has brought us up against various obstacles, but the story of evolution reminds us that we advance when there is a problem to overcome. Some of these obstacles have been challenges that faced, and continue to face, all human life. Others are more personal.

The story of the Fall illustrates the universal tendency to pass the blame for every misstep or deliberate misconduct onto someone else. The blame culture is a chain, blocking the path to becoming the best we can be, because it blinds us to our own need to change and to learn from our mistakes. Instead we become ensnared in an attitude of defensiveness and litigation that can ultimately stop us taking any risks or any responsibility. It stops us growing up. In what ways do you see this chain at work in your own life or in our world today?

The incident with the Golden Calf warns us how easy it is to let impatience tempt us to settle for shoddy imitations and fraudulent fakes when our heart's true quest seeks the gold standard of truth and authenticity. Are there any golden calves in your life and your world today? Can you name them and shame them?

Our newspapers and social media bristle with easy judgements and prejudiced assumptions. We are widely exposed to shameless propaganda operating subliminally on the way we see our neighbour, our country and our world. How quick are you to stand in judgement? How ready are you, like Nathanael, to dismiss others because of where they come from, how they look, speak or conduct their lives? Our readiness to judge each other is a constantly recurring stumbling block on our journey.

Our gifts, on the other hand, are sometimes all too easily dismissed, or hidden away unused, to gather dust. On our spiritual journey are we more concerned with being 'saved' than being 'spent'? How do you feel about the warning 'Use it or lose it', in connection with your personal giftedness?

And then that question: 'Who is my neighbour?' We feel we are already on overload – information overload – compassion fatigue. Small wonder that we often react with a shrug – 'not my problem'. But what does the story of the good Samaritan ask of us? What does Love ask of us?

Do any of these obstacles speak especially to you today? Have you encountered any of them? What other obstacles would you add to the discussion?

The story of Zacchaeus, however, can lead us gently from the challenge of obstacles to the consolation of encouragement, because Jesus tells him, 'Come down. I'm coming home with you today.' Such a prospect might have us worrying about the state of the bathroom and the neglected washing-up, but Zacchaeus responds, we hear, by 'welcoming him joyfully'.

Can we do the same, as we move on to reflect on the abundance of encouragement we encounter along our soul journey?

FOURTH WEEK OF LENT

Fresh Springs

MONDAY
God is in this place

*Jacob left Beersheba and set out for Haran. When he
had reached a certain place, he stopped there for the night,
since the sun had set. He took one of the stones of that place,
made it his pillow and lay down where he was. He had a dream:
there was a ladder, planted on the ground with its top
reaching to heaven; and on it were God's angels, going up
and down. And there was the Lord, standing over him and saying,
'I am the Lord, the God of Abraham your father, and
the God of Isaac.... Then Jacob awoke from his sleep and said,
'Truly, the Lord is in this place and I did not know!'
(Genesis 28:10-13, 16)*

You may be feeling a bit like Jacob, after a week of surmounting
obstacles along the journey. He seems to be weary beyond
exhaustion as night falls, but all he can find by way of a pillow
is a stone he finds on the wayside. And there he sleeps, and
dreams. We are probably all familiar with his famous dream.
Jacob's Ladder has given its name to many places, climbs and
hiking trails all over the world. In Jacob's dream the ladder
connects heaven and earth and is populated by angels ascending
and descending. As in all dreams, the symbols visualised are
expressions of something stirring in the deeper levels of
consciousness, normally inaccessible to rational enquiry.

A friend surprised us once, while we were sharing our
various responses to Jacob's dream. She sat quietly throughout
our conversation and we were aware that she was going deep.
She had had more than her fair share of problems. In a terrible
accident she had been badly injured, and had been confined to

a wheelchair ever since. Following the accident her husband had decided that he wasn't able or willing to care for her for the rest of their lives, and left her for another partner. Her journey since then had been a stony road, with no bright star on the horizon, no close companionship to support her, and very little by way of encouragement to keep going.

But keep going she did, with a fortitude and patience that amazed us. Those who knew and loved her stepped in whenever possible, to give her what help they could. But through the long days of struggle and the even longer lonely nights, she slept, you might say, on a pillow of stone.

As our gathering was drawing to a close we noticed the tears in her eyes. 'This is my story,' she said. 'And this is my ladder. My friends go up and come down like angels when I really need them. But more than anything else I realise now that this place in life, this stony ground, is the very place where the ladder that connects me to God begins. God is in this place, here and now, and I never knew it until today.'

It was a very moving moment. We tend to assume that moments when we feel especially close to the holy mystery usually spring from experiences of joy and peace. But for our friend and for Jacob, that ladder of connection was grounded in the stony ground, the long hard walk through hostile terrain.

I was once travelling on the ferry across the Irish Sea from Dublin in Ireland to Holyhead in Wales. It was a night crossing, and the full moon was riding high in the midnight sky. I stood on the deck, thinking back to Ireland and my sadness at leaving. As I looked out across the dark expanse of water, I saw a silver pathway stretching all the way from the boat to the shores of Ireland. And I knew that wherever I might have been standing, whether on the boat or on shore, or along any part of the coastline, that moonlight path would start from exactly where I was and lead directly to where I longed to be. It is a phenomenon you can observe on any moonlit night on seashore or lakeside, but for me it is always my 'Jacob's carpet'.

We don't have to go to somewhere special or remote to

find the beginning of our heart's connection to God. It always begins exactly where we are, whether the ground is smooth or stony. God assures Jacob that this sacred presence who speaks into his dreaming is the God of his ancestors, the God of all time and our connection to all eternity, planted firmly on our home ground and reaching all the way to heaven – our destiny.

Dreams only become meaningful when we wake up and live them into reality. My friend's attitude to her own painful situation only changed when she was able to say – and to really *know* – that 'God is in this place and I never knew it.' Jacob subsequently took the stone he had been using as a pillow and set it up as a marker stone, a permanent reminder, a touchstone that reveals the presence of what is most precious and can never be lost because it travels with us, wherever we go.

Pause ...

... to ask for the grace to discover the sacred presence wherever, and however, we are, and not to waste our energy trying to find it anywhere else.

TUESDAY
Water into wine

There were six stone water jars there, in accordance
with the purification rites of the Jews: each could hold about
a hundred litres. Jesus said to them, 'Fill the jars with water,'
and they filled them to the brim. Then he said to them, 'Now
draw some out and take it to the president of the feast.' They
took it. When the president tasted the water that had become
wine ... he called the bridegroom and said, 'Everyone serves
good wine first and the less good wine when the guests have
drunk deep; but you have kept the best wine till now.'
(John 2:6-10)

Jesus, his friends and his mother are guests at a wedding feast. The wine runs out and Jesus' mother prompts him to do something about it. Jesus is reluctant – even resistant – to her prompting, but she insists, telling the servants to do whatever he tells them to do.

Other key factors in this drama are the stone water jars. Jesus instructs the servants to fill these with water and then draw off some of the water and take it to the steward to taste. The steward, however, tastes not water but wine – and the best wine of the night.

This is the gist of this very familiar story – known as Jesus' first miracle, but what does it mean for us personally, and how does it encourage us as we navigate our soul journey?

It begins with emptiness. The water jars are empty before the transformation process begins. Emptiness holds the potential for transformation. Most of us experience many periods in our lives when we feel empty, drained, and useless and it can feel like the end of the road. Henry David Thoreau even suggested that 'most people live lives of quiet desperation' so if we feel like this we are not alone. In our times there is also a collective sense of desperation and a loss of direction.

How does this gospel story offer us encouragement in such times? Here are a few suggestions.

First, emptiness is a place of transformation. Sometimes we need to be emptied out before we can be filled with something new. Emptiness is not something to be feared, but perhaps rather a space for hope and possibility.

It's clear that the water jars can't fill themselves up, and neither can we. It needs an outside agency. All we, or the water jars, can do is provide empty, receptive space. Receptivity is key. All that is needed is the simplest of elements – H_2O, ordinary water. Often it is the ordinary things in life that fill our emptiness if we are receptive to them. Perhaps something from the natural world, or from what we read or hear or the warmth of friendship makes us feel more alive. Try looking back over each day and noticing what has poured something life-giving into your jar today.

There is also a real need for trust that things can change. In fact, change is the only constant in our lives. Everything is changing all the time, and we can truly trust that 'this too shall pass'.

Finally, we need to trust the pouring out. However firmly we believe that all we contain is water, others may receive it as wine that will change their lives. This can apply to something as simple as a friendly gesture or as major as a decision to change course in some way. Don't let us store up our vital energy 'for a rainy day', when the challenge might be to spend it here and now, and trust that it will always be replenished.

The miracle of water into wine is happening all the time in every vineyard, but it takes years. Over time the water that feeds the vine is transformed, inside the vine, into wine. We are the vines, and our lives are the spaces where ordinary everyday experience is transformed, gradually, and through prayerful reflection, into wine that can be life-giving for others.

There could be a little twist to the tale: imagine yourself back in Cana. The steward, who has seen nothing of the procedure with the water jars, is given the new wine to taste. He is *expecting* wine. What he is not expecting is that this wine will be the finest of all, far exceeding what has been offered before. Now imagine yourself among those guests who *did* witness what happened with the water jars. They will be expecting water to be drawn out, given that water was poured in. Perhaps they got water! Another miracle worth pondering is that when we expect nothing to happen, nothing may well happen, but if we are open – receptive – to new possibilities, this is what we will discover.

And, possibly most encouraging of all, sometimes the best wine is saved to the last. Maybe your later years will yield the finest fruit. Can you trust that? Perhaps you can already see the evidence? You may be mainly conscious of the diminishment of advancing age, but what about the life wisdom that has evolved out of all your experience? Could that be the difference between the *vin de table* of your early years and the finest vintage of your later life?

Pause ...

... to ask for the grace to trust that our emptiness can become a place of transformation and that what we perceive as diminishment may actually be our life's true harvest time.

WEDNESDAY

Lost sheep

*'What do you think? If a man has a hundred sheep and
one of them strays; will he not leave the ninety-nine in the
mountains and go in search of the stray? Amen I say to you,
if he finds it, he rejoices more over it than over the ninety-nine
that did not stray. Similarly, it is never the will of your Father
in heaven that one of these little ones should be lost.'*
(Matthew 18:12-14)

Paul is a paramedic in Scotland. He flies to remote locations
in the Highlands and Islands, conveying critically ill patients
to mainland hospitals or carrying out rescue missions for the
seriously injured who need helicopter transport.

One day he was called out to a drowning incident. Several
people had drowned and a little girl was in a critical condition.
When the team arrived on scene, it became obvious that the
child needed urgent specialist care, but she was too unstable
for air transport. The paramedics alerted the mainland, and a
team of off-duty paediatric specialists was called in. Specialist
life support equipment was flown to the scene of the accident,
along with the hastily assembled medical team. Together
medics and paramedics worked all through the night to save
the child's life.

Back home, he first gave his daughters a big hug, dismissing
their excited praise, then said simply 'It's all about the patient.
If we can't get the patient to the hospital, we will move heaven
and earth to take the hospital to the patient.' That night Paul
and all his colleagues shared in the joy that the one lost sheep
had been found.

It always amazes me just how much trouble ordinary human beings will take to rescue those in difficulty, including animals. How many kittens have got stuck down drains or in treetops? How many injured dogs have been brought back to life against all the odds? Recently the workers in a Sydney office in Australia called out the animal rescue service to extract a tiny bird who had flown into an obscure corner of an area of the building. It took a long time, but the bird was rescued, revived, and eventually flew free, to the great delight of the office staff, who likewise shared in the joy of the 'one who was found'.

In December 2004 the Asian tsunami claimed almost a quarter of a million human lives. At the time a supply ship was at sea off the Thai coast. The crew were aware of the huge swell, but their boat was able to ride it out. A few days later they noticed something floating on the water just about within sight of their boat. Closer investigation revealed what looked like a body draped over a large piece of driftwood. Immediately they dropped all their plans and headed out on their own rescue mission.

Soon a twelve-year-old girl was lying on the deck, wrapped in blankets and just beginning to return to consciousness. She had been swept out to sea by the force of the tsunami, and had clung to a piece of wood for several days, drifting closer and closer to what seemed like inevitable death. Now she was safe, but there was another problem. As she began to speak, none of the international crew could understand her language. Then the captain himself knelt down beside her and to everyone's amazement he discovered that both he and the child were Norwegian and were able to communicate with each other in their own language.

What are the chances of being rescued from a tsunami and by someone who speaks your own minority language? The news of the rescue of the little girl was rapidly texted around everyone who worked for the ship's company and the burly seafarers who made up the crew of this vessel, as well as their colleagues who had been on shore at the time, broke down in tears of joy as they heard the news that this little lost soul had been restored to life.

Perhaps today we might hold in thought and prayer, and be deeply encouraged by, all those who live the story of the lost sheep in our own time and place: the emergency services, and all the ordinary folk who care enough to passionately seek out the ones who are lost, hurt or at risk and bring them home, often at great cost to their own safety and comfort.

Pause ...

... to ask for the grace to care enough to leave our comfort zone and go in search of the 'little ones' of whom God wills that none should be lost.

THURSDAY
Water from the rock

*Moses cried out to the Lord for help, saying 'What am I
to do with this people? They are almost ready to stone me!'
Then the Lord said to Moses, 'Go on ahead of the people,
taking some of the elders of Israel with you; in your hand take
the staff with which you struck the river, and go. I shall be
waiting for you there on the rock (at Horeb). Strike the rock,
and water will come out for the people to drink.'
(Exodus 17:4-6)*

Moses is in an impossible situation, not for the first time in the
long saga of the exodus of the children of Israel from Egypt.
The water has run out again and the people are demanding to
know why he has led them into the desert only to let them die
of thirst. Yet again Moses turns to God in his desperation, and
God's response sounds improbable, to say the least. Striking a
rockface with a stick hardly sounds very scientific, but Moses
is a man of faith.

It was a sunny September morning in downtown Manhattan.
A young woman made her commuter journey to the hospital
where she worked as a neurological assessment nurse. As she
emerged from the subway a low-flying aircraft collided with one
of the twin towers of the World Trade Centre. She quickened
her pace. This had the making of a terrible accident and it was
going to be a busy day. Before she could make it to her place of
work the bizarre scene repeated itself, as a second aircraft hit
the second tower. From then on she was aware of little more
than the fevered activity of the assessment department and the
ash clouds that now shrouded the whole area.

Seated in front of her was a young black man covered in grey ash and totally mute. Her task was to assess whether he was 'just' in shock or if there was evidence of neurological damage, but the patient showed no flicker of response, no body language, no eye contact, nothing. At this point she may well have been feeling like Moses, quite unable to see any way forward, yet desperately sorry for the young man in front of her.

Then something quite unplanned occurred. As she observed her patient with a feeling of increasing helplessness, a single tear rolled across his cheek, tracing a shiny black river through two banks of the ash that covered his skin. On an impulse of compassion, and contrary to all the normal guidelines, she stretched out her hand and with a gentle finger, she touched the tear. This was all that was needed. Then the tears flowed freely like that stream in the wilderness released by the touch of Moses' stick. With the flood of tears the story also flowed free. The patient had been in his office with a colleague. The plane hit, and he dived underneath the desk. His colleague was not so quick and lost his life.

Most of us feel caught up in impossible situations from time to time and can see no way forward, no way out. Nothing, it seems, can break through the impasse except a miracle. And quite frankly the hope of a miracle is as unlikely as the story of Moses getting water from a rock. Or is it?

When I feel like this, I remember that it was just an insignificant little stick that Moses used to draw water from the rock, and it was just one slender finger that drew forth the floods of grief and pain that would make possible the beginning of healing for the young man in Manhattan. It was the power of faith that overcame the hard rock in the desert. It was the power of compassion that overcame the mute desperation of a victim of terrorism in downtown Manhattan.

These two stories, one from long ago, the other from painfully recent times are messages of encouragement along our path. Not because we are likely to be offered a magic remedy to solve our problems, but because they show us that miracles usually come in very small packages and that they happen most frequently when we are at the end of our own resources. Moses could do nothing in his own strength but had to rely solely on his trust that a breakthrough could happen in ways beyond his power or comprehension. The Manhattan nurse could do nothing medically to break the impasse of her patient's state of shock, but was able only to reach out in a simple gesture of human compassion. Our own helplessness, alongside a tiny space for faith, a fleeting opportunity to show compassion, these are the cracks in our human management of things that, in the words of Leonard Cohen, allow the light to get in.

Pause ...

... to ask for the grace to keep believing that the solid walls of all that seems impossible are the very place where we will find the little doors of unexpected possibilities.

FRIDAY
Let down

*Some men came, bringing on a bed a paralysed man
whom they were trying to bring in and lay down in front
of Jesus. But as they could find no way of getting the man
through the crowd, they went up onto the top of the house
and lowered him and his stretcher down through the tiles
into the middle, in front of Jesus.*
(Luke 5:18-19)

This has always been a favourite gospel incident of mine. It's so easy to imagine the throng of people surrounding the house where they know Jesus is to be found. His reputation as a healer goes ahead of him now, and there's no avoiding the celebrity, however unwanted it may be. Everyone wants a piece of the action.

This is a story about determination and breaking down barriers when they come between ourselves and what our hearts most long for. This paralysed man has friends who are prepared to go to extreme lengths to get him the help they believe he needs. When they can't get through the crowds, they take him up onto the roof, rip the tiles apart and lower him down until he is lying exactly where they wanted him to be – at the feet of Jesus

These friends think they are facing an impossible task to get him close to Jesus, until they hit on the idea of letting him down through the roof. *They let him down.* Just ponder those four simple words. Being let down is what we very much dislike. We trust our friends *not* to let us down. We hope we wouldn't let *them* down. But whenever I re-visit this gospel scene it is the act of letting down that fires my imagination. Of course it's just a play on words, but even so it reminds me that often enough, when life lets me down, by failing to meet my hopes and expectations, this is precisely what brings me to a place I would otherwise never have arrived at. Perhaps it forces me to see things differently, to review my options and take a different course, or to discover resources I never knew I had.

Often enough it is life itself that 'lets us down'. Maybe illness strikes or we experience a serious loss or disappointment or institutions we have always trusted prove to be untrustworthy. Have you had an experience like this? How did you move on from it? What did you learn from it? Did it perhaps hold a hidden gift that you couldn't recognise at the time but that has opened up something new and life-giving for you?

I am also tremendously encouraged by the fact that the friends of the paralytic actually destroyed part of the roof. Jesus' reaction to this is not recorded, but somehow I can't imagine these 'vandals' receiving a sharp letter from Jesus' solicitor or a bill for damages. I guess I wouldn't be very happy if someone ripped any of my tiles away, but Jesus has different priorities. His concern is to heal the man who has broken through so many barriers to get to him.

Just what form do those barriers take for us? What is paralysing us? For many of us the current political situation seems paralysed. We feel helpless as we watch things being said and done that in no way reflect our own deeply held values and principles. When such a situation becomes extreme it can cause the old political structures to break down as people vote with their feet, abandoning old tribal loyalties in the search for something radically new. This doesn't mean they are giving up on democracy but rather seeking to revitalise it.

A similar paralysis can afflict religious systems and structures and here, too, large numbers of people are voting with their feet and relinquishing their allegiance to the traditional denominations and faith systems. This doesn't mean they are abandoning their spiritual journey, but possibly exploring fresh channels through which their spiritual quest can flow.

The friends in the story decide that to move beyond the paralysis they need to break down what is obstructing their quest, and sometimes we also have to break through, or break down what is impeding our soul journey. Some would even say that Jesus himself, and his simple yet all-powerful message has become so overlaid with man-made accretions and regulations that they no longer recognise him through the disguises that formal religion has laid upon him.

What, if anything is paralysing *you*? Is there anything you need to break down in order to approach what really matters most to you? Let this story encourage you to be bold and determined, letting nothing make Jesus inaccessible to you.

Pause ...

... to ask for the grace of trust when we feel let down and courage to break through whatever barriers come between us and the God who makes us whole.

SATURDAY
The crushed reed

Here is my servant whom I uphold,
My chosen one in whom my soul delights.
I have put my spirit upon him,
he will bring fair judgement to the nations.
He will not cry out or raise his voice,
his voice will not be heard in the street.
A crushed reed he will not break
nor will he snuff out a faltering wick.
(Isaiah 42:1-3)

Right now, our hearts are crying out, audibly, for the fulfilment of this promise. What would we give to have leadership that is guided by such a spirit as this. With what relief would we vote for one who would not just promise to bring fair judgement to the nations, but actually deliver on the promise? Can we really be encouraged by the divine promise offered in today's reading? Can we trust it, when we have come dangerously close to losing all trust in anyone or anything in our troubled times?

The prophet gives us a thumbnail sketch of what such a leader would be like. This would be a calm and quiet person who doesn't rant and rave or blast us with bombastic rhetoric. We don't hear him shouting in the streets, or on the airwaves or on social media. She is sensitive, taking care not to damage further what is already hurting. He doesn't write tendentious columns in the press or make fiery speeches to whip up hostility against other nations or against minorities in his own land. She doesn't cut off the oxygen from the flickering flames of hope or muzzle the almost inaudible appeals of the poor for justice.

While this description of how a leader of integrity would behave reminds me painfully of how far we are from having such leadership, it also encourages me, because if we can imagine it, we can make it happen. Again and again scripture holds out to us the ideal and invites us to imagine making it reality. In fact, this is a guiding theme of our soul journey. In Jesus of Nazareth we see what our best looks like, in a human life lived on planet Earth. But if this seems too far beyond achievement, let's see where else we see glimpses of it, in people and events around us that show us aspects of this portrait of spirit-led leadership.

Here are some glimpses of 'living our best life' in unexpected places. These are people who, like the prototype described by Isaiah, tend to be quiet and unobtrusive, not making waves but helping us to swim, not likely to feature in the tabloids, but quite possibly known only to their immediate friends and neighbours.

Here are the parents whose small child has just been diagnosed with a rare and aggressive childhood cancer. They sit at her bedside day and night, playing with her and distracting her from the torment of the chemotherapy. They will never give up on her. They will keep fanning the flickering flames of hope in their child and in each other, and they are helped in this by the tenderness and skilled care of the medical staff.

And here comes a schoolgirl on her way home from class. She's a bit of a troublemaker, a teenage rebel. Her school uniform is worn as provocatively as possible, but she stops to speak to a homeless man. It's obviously not the first time. They chat like old friends and she brings them both a coffee. For a precious ten minutes his spirits rise, and he feels alive again. Life has crushed him, but a word of kindness relieves the pain.

A little child is howling as if the world were ending. She has let go of her balloon string and now it is floating off across the road, likely to be burst by the next car that passes but the next car that passes stops. The driver gets out. He goes to pick up the wayward balloon, just in time before it flies away. He crosses the road and gives it back to the wailing child, whose sorrow turns at once to joy.

It's waste disposal day, and the bins will be collected soon. It's also a witheringly hot day and the heatwave shows no sign of abating. One of the bins has a little note attached. Maybe someone has something to complain about. It wouldn't be anything unusual in the current fractious atmosphere. But when I get close enough to read it I discover instead the words: 'If you could use a cool drink of water please call here.' I can surely hear Jesus murmuring from the roadside: 'Anyone who gives so much as a cup of cold water to one of these little ones … will most certainly not go without the reward' (Matthew 10:42).

As I recall these glimpses of goodness, I realise that I could fill a book with them – and so, I'm sure, could you. I also realise that I will find them much more readily by looking around me at the ordinary people, living their best lives in their own way, than in a futile search for integrity in the higher echelons of power.

Pause …

… to ask for the grace to recognise the glimpses of goodness all around us as little pebbles of encouragement scattered along our way to guide us closer to the best we can be.

SABBATH PAUSE
A grain of sand

*For you the weight of the whole world in the scales is
like a drop of morning dew falling on the ground.
... You love all that exists.*
(Wisdom 11:22,24)

At the end of a week during which we have been refreshed
at various fresh springs of encouragement, we slow down and
take stock again, to draw on all our reserves for the coming
week, with its new and perhaps demanding rocky climbs and
spiritual challenges.

But first a sabbath pause. These words from the book of
Wisdom are clearly intended to contrast the infinite power of
God with the relative frailty and flimsiness of our world and
all it contains.

A publisher friend, when asked what his work vision is,
says that he hopes he might help to 'tip the world just a little
in the direction of the best we can be'. That sounds to me
like a vision worth living by, a star worth following. When we
reflect on the sheer vastness of the known universe, and the
observation that if every *galaxy* (which itself contains billions
of stars) were the size of a frozen pea, those peas would fill
the Albert Hall in London, we get a sense of our own apparent
insignificance. But what if each one of us, insignificant though
we feel ourselves to be, has the ability to 'tip the scales' of the
human spirit a little bit closer towards the best it can be?

I was once in a cemetery in South Wales, reflecting on
the life of a friend who had passed and had left her own very
beautiful mark on Earth. I noticed the sunlight glinting on the

grass, making the dewdrops sparkle like diamonds and I asked myself which would I rather be – a diamond or a dewdrop. I decided that a dewdrop is the better choice. A diamond is for ever, so they say, and a dewdrop is gone by noon, but in that time it has soaked into the earth and nourished new life in a way no diamond ever can.

So today, let us pause to consider the great gift we have – the Power of One. Each of us is only one among billions of earth-dwellers, and Earth herself is only one among billions of planets circling billions of stars among billions of galaxies. Yet we have this amazing gift —the power of One. You may be surprised to learn that the butterfly has it too. We call it the Butterfly Effect. This means that, for example, when a butterfly flaps her wings in Indonesia the change in air pressure, amplified by feedback loops, can become a force strong enough to cause a tornado in Kentucky. Put more generally, it means that an infinitesimally small change in initial conditions can grow, through successive feedback loops into a world-changing force.

Christians might see this pattern reflected in an insignificant birth in an unregarded region of the Middle East to unknown parents, marking the advent of a baby who would grow up to tell the world a new story about God – or rather, a new chapter of an ancient story, and this story would grow, by being retold and lived out in successive generations, into a story to change the world. The most important changes in the human story begin from tiny seeds and each one of us is such a seed. The new story that this baby tells is a love story, about a God who 'loves everything that exists'.

You might like to take some time today to reflect on the places of encouragement we have visited this week. Which of them has spoken to your condition? Are there any you would add, perhaps favourite texts or memories? How might your own life, your words, choices, actions, help to tip the scales a little bit towards the best we can be? Do you believe in your own Power of One?

When a butterfly emerges from the chrysalis the very first

thing she does is lie in the sun and dry her wings, soaking up solar energy for the next chapter of her life. How often do you pause to 'dry your wings' and simply soak up the energy of life, doing nothing, receiving everything? Far from being a waste of time, as we in the west have been conditioned to believe, it is the perfect way to make a sabbath pause.

Rocky Crags

MONDAY
The cliffs of conflict

They will hammer their swords into ploughshares
and their spears into sickles.
Nation will not lift sword against nation;
No longer will they learn to make war.
(Isaiah 2:4)

This sounds like a resolution passed by the United Nations, and the inner cynic suggests that it will never really be implemented. Yet it is what almost everyone on Earth longs for. At the turn of the millennium TV coverage followed the dawn of the new age through Earth's time zones from east to west, and the universal desire for the dawn of a new beginning was for peace. The vast majority of Earth-dwellers just long to be able to live their lives, till their fields and raise their families without the ever-present threat of conflict. But what chance of Isaiah's vision ever becoming a reality?

In 1992, long-festering racial injustice erupted in Los Angeles. The streets of LA turned into rivers of rage. Children growing up in that period lost their childhood and learned to survive – or not – in a war zone. Gang membership flourished and gang violence increased exponentially.

In 1994 a young and inexperienced teacher, Erin Gruwell, joined the staff of the Woodrow Wilson High School in California. Racial tensions ran high, and her first class – young people who had already been written off as inevitable dropouts – were deeply embroiled in the gang culture that had shaped them. They sat in hostile confrontation with each other – the African-Americans, the Latinos, the Asians and the East Europeans. Open conflict erupted at the slightest provocation. Guns, inevitably, were in easy reach. An intractable situation, exposing the deep-running tensions that exist everywhere between different groups of human beings.

One day Erin invited them to form two lines, facing each other. She drew a chalk line between them. With expressions of derision they formed lines reflecting their gang allegiances.

'Step up to the line,' she said, 'if you like ...' and she named a well-known rapper. Most of them stepped up to the line, keeping their eyes lowered.

'Step up to the line if you belong to a gang.' Almost everyone shuffled up to the line, eyes still lowered.

'Step up to the line if you have been shot at, or lost someone you loved, to gang violence.' Most of them stepped up, some raising their eyes in fury to meet the eyes of someone from the rival gang responsible for that death.

'Stay at the line if you have lost more than one friend to gang violence.' At least half of them stayed at the line.

And so it continued until a few students still stood at the line, having lost four or more friends. 'Let's now just honour the memory of all of these people. Call out their names as we do so.' The classroom resounded with the names of young children, teenagers, brothers, sisters, parents, friends. Everyone in the class had stood face to face with another person, from a rival gang, who had suffered the same senseless loss. This was the beginning of a huge transformation.

The teacher went on to introduce the class to stories of other young people in the world, also caught up in inherited tribal violence. Through her tireless efforts she empowered them to change their lives, to hammer their swords into ploughshares or, in this case, their guns into keyboards, as, under her guidance, they began to tell their stories and explore their lives, hopes and dreams in what became The Freedom Writers' Diaries. This project, that began in a class of teenagers who had been largely written off by the education system, became a catalyst for change in teaching methods in their own country and internationally.

Back in Europe and it's Christmas 1914. A brief ceasefire

has been declared along the western front. From behind the 'enemy' lines the sounds of Christmas carols can be heard. The soldiers emerge from the trenches, incredulous that the guns are stilled. A football match begins in no-man's land. Small gifts and mementos are exchanged between 'friend' and 'foe'. You can't do any of that without looking into the other person's eyes and once you have looked into another person's eyes and seen the unique, vulnerable human being inside, can you then go on to kill them? This was clear to the generals, of course, who very rapidly called off the ceasefire. If it had continued for just a few days more, the course of twentieth century history might have been completely changed.

What can we learn in all of this? Two powerful lessons emerge. The first is that peace begins on the ground floor where we live our lives, and not from the rooftop where those who govern us reside. The second is that this 'ground floor' peace begins when we look into the eyes of those we have been conditioned to see as 'the enemy' and see instead another human being who loves, dreams, hopes, fears and grieves just as we do ourselves.

Is there any source of conflict in your own neighbourhood that is in need of some transformation? Can you forge any personal link that might turn a sword into a ploughshare – a word or act of hostility into a word or act that fosters new understanding?

Pause ...

... to ask for the grace to dare to look into our enemy's eyes and see another human being, so that the no-man's land of temporary ceasefire may become everyman's land of lasting peace.

TUESDAY
The caves of confusion

*They reached the territory of the Gerasenes on the other
side of the lake, and when he disembarked, a man with an
unclean spirit at once came out from the tombs towards him.
The man lived among the tombs and no one could secure him
any more, even with a cord because he had often been secured
with fetters and cords but had snapped the cords and rubbed away
the fetters, and no one had the strength to control him.
All night and all day, among the tombs and in the mountains,
he was howling and gashing himself with stones. … Then Jesus
asked, 'What is your name?' He answered, 'My name is Legion,
for there are many of us.'*
(Mark 5:1-9)

During a hiking holiday in the far north west of Scotland,
a friend and I had a mysterious encounter. The landscape
was utterly deserted heathland. My friend, normally calm and
rational, suddenly announced 'We are not alone'. I thought
he had caught a touch of the sun, as our solitude was beyond
dispute. And then a figure rather like the man in today's
story rose up out of the heather. He was wild and lived
in the caves, only making his way to the nearest centre of
population once a week to claim his welfare benefits. All
attempts to control him and bring him into the circle of
civilisation had failed.

We discovered that he had been a paratrooper during the
war and was dropped behind enemy lines where he had been
severely traumatised. He was not above visiting the kirk when
he came for his benefit money, and helping himself to the

collection, as well as to the Bibles and hymn books to make a fire when he got back to his cave.

In the light of this adventure, the story of the Gerasene demoniac comes across as a little less bizarre than may at first appear. There are many people living on the margins of our society today who are barely subsisting and are snarled up in a knot of anger, confusion and desperation no less than the man from the land of the Gerasenes. No one is listening to them. They have been wiped from the social radar and left to howl their protests to the heavens. Society doesn't know how to handle them.

He tells Jesus his name is 'legion', because 'there are many' of him. We might express this feeling as being 'all over the place'. In today's world we face a legion of chaotic and bewildering developments that threaten to overwhelm us. Inwardly we may also be screaming and howling and even self-harming. Indeed, in Britain we are collectively harming ourselves in a subconscious attempt to get some control of situations in which we feel unheard and invisible.

There are very many aspects of modern life that can feel terrifying. Each one alone is a huge challenge, but together they seem like the end of life as we know it. We may well feel overwhelmed, for example, by the rapid and often intrusive force of technology, or impotent in the face of impending climate change, or disenfranchised by our political systems and overruled by decisions that we judge to be unwise or downright wrong.

What does 'legion' mean for *you*? And how do we find a way forward when we feel locked into a place of helplessness, anger and frustration. An intrepid old lady once gave me an object lesson …

It was a warm summer Saturday afternoon in the main shopping street of a large northern city. There had been a big football match, and the fans were streaming down the street like a human tsunami, alcohol- and testosterone-fuelled, high on victory or furious over defeat, threatening to crush everything in their path. Startled shoppers took cover in shop doorways to avoid being trampled. It was a terrifying experience.

One elderly lady was caught in mid-flow but before anyone could take steps to rescue her, she turned round to face the onslaught, and singled out just one individual teenage boy from the melee. She held him by the shoulders and he turned to jelly in her grip. The confidence of the herd deserted him. Now he was on his own, facing this formidable opposition. What if the same logic applies to our problems? Collectively they seem insuperable, but what if we take just one strand at a time? Each single strand of anxiety might be much more easily dealt with.

The sequel to this strange story is that Jesus casts out the demons and sends them into a herd of pigs, who then destroy themselves by hurtling off a cliff. It has been wisely observed that if we fail to process our anger we will pass it on, and the negative energy will play itself out in other, even more far-reaching ways. If we don't transform the negative energy, we will transmit it. The pig incident may be more relevant to our present condition than it might appear.

Take a few moments to reflect on your own state of mind at present. Do you ever feel a surge of impotent anger or the frustration of having little or no control over what is happening in your life, your country or the world? Can you let Jesus approach you and talk with you in your prayer as he talked with the Gerasene demoniac? Does this prayer encounter help you discover any path through the maze of your confusion?

Pause ...

... to ask for the grace to let the Holy Spirit hover over our chaos and confusion, embrace our brokenness and draw it towards healing, one strand at a time.

WEDNESDAY
The rockface of ageing

... when you were young
you put on your own belt
and walked where you liked;
but when you grow old
you will stretch out your hands,
and someone else will put a belt round you
and take you where you would rather not go.
(John 21:18)

I'm so grateful that I can still walk where I like, being blessed with good health and full mobility, and one of my favourite walks is around the paths and field tracks surrounding the semi-rural community where I live. Every time I walk there, I see change. In spring the fields show just a haze of green, signalling new growth and the season of youth. Soon the tender fresh green darkens into summer verdure, but with it come the stinging nettles and the path gets overgrown. Adult life reflected in nature.

Autumn arrives, and the crops have been harvested. The field is just an expanse of stubble. The paths become water-logged when the storms break, and I can't always walk where I like. The season of ageing is here. The plough goes through the field, leaving everything bare, yet the fresh-made furrows have a beauty of their own. The first frosts arrive. Walking gets more hazardous, but the trees reveal the beauty of their unadorned branches against a winter sunset. Beneath my feet a new year is sleeping. It will awaken when the season is right, perhaps not for me, but for those who will walk these paths when I am gone.

Growing old is not for the faint-hearted. Even if we retain our health into our older years, the anxieties mount. How will we finance age care if we need it? How can we avoid becoming a burden to our children? How will we cope with loss and diminishment, sickness or incapacity? Will we lose our independence? What will our lives amount to, and will the world be any better for our having been here? There are plenty of boulders blocking the path.

A wise elder once reminded me: 'Memory is a paradise from which we can never be evicted.' As I enter the final chapter of my life I don't want 'memory' just to be some kind of delusional nostalgia, like having a sentimental magazine to read while I linger in the departure hall, waiting for my flight to be called. And I don't want it to mean a constant state of regret that I can't do the things I used to do, or that I will never again visit the places that I have loved. Dwelling on the things that are gone and won't come back is a fast track to dejection and despair. Memories can then become like stinging nettles. It hurts, just to think of them, and that's no kind of paradise.

A more fruitful approach to the paradise of memory might be to reflect on all that our life has brought us, as we distil the wisdom from it, and perhaps also to pass on this wisdom to the next generation. In many cultures the elders are regarded as the main repository of life wisdom and are respected and cherished. The young seek them out, for guidance on their own life journeys. In the west we all too often settle our elders in care homes and assume that they are past their sell-by date. Our young people will not automatically turn to us with their life questions, but when we are gone they may wish they had. I certainly regret not spending more time in my youth listening to the wealth of experience of my own elders. One way to offer them this experience is to write about it for them, or to record your memories in some way that they can re-visit when they are ready to do so.

In today's reading, John speaks of the pain of dependency. After a life lived in the mainstream it can be hard to accept, let alone ask for, help. In any care home there will be residents who resent any perceived interference in their daily routines, and others who have learned the art of gracious, grateful acceptance of the help, companionship and kindness offered by others. It seems to be our own attitudes that determine whether memory becomes a prison or a paradise.

Jesus never grew old. But in the days ahead of us on this journey we will learn a great deal from him about how to embrace loss and diminishment. He will even guide us down the paths we most dread – the loss of friends, the loss of dignity, and ultimately the loss of life itself. And he will show us how death – whether the death of our bodies or of our hopes and dreams – is never extinction, but always transformation. All of the natural world assures of this. When all seems dead in winter, we know that life is simply sleeping and will rise again in spring. How could we possibly be an exception to this universal natural law? Life and death are not adversaries, but partners in the great dance of life.

Pause ...

.... to ask for the grace, when we come to the end of our earthly road, to be able to say, 'I'm glad I did', and not 'I wish I had.'

THURSDAY
The chasms between generations

'No one puts a piece of unshrunken cloth onto an old cloak,
because the patch pulls away from the cloak and a worse
tear happens. Nor do people put new wine into old wineskins;
otherwise, the skins burst, the wine runs out, and the skins
are lost. No, they put new wine into fresh skins and
both are preserved.'
(Matthew 9:16-17)

You can't put old heads on young shoulders, so they say. Nor can you put young heads on old shoulders, much as we might welcome a brain transplant as we grow older and more forgetful. The image in today's reading, of a patch of new cloth tearing away from an old garment is very vivid. It brings to mind the word *tearaway*, too often used to criticise the behaviour of the young. The image of new wine bursting out of an old wineskin also comes close to home when we think of the outbursts of frustration and resentment that so often mar our family relationships.

Jesus could have been talking here about conflict between generations, and one of the big challenges of our time is the problem of inter-generational injustice. I consider that I drew a good hand in the gamble of life. I was born right at the end of a period of war, enjoyed the benefits of an excellent education, through school and university, at no cost to my parents, as well as world-class 'cradle-to-grave' health care, free to everyone at the point of need. I left education to enter a buoyant employment market, which enabled me, in my twenties, to have my own home, albeit with a mortgage. In spite of various redundancy alarms, employment crises and economic recessions, I, along with my generation, survived and now have the benefit of a state pension.

My grandchildren, on the other hand, are growing up in times of extreme instability, will have to pay heavily for tertiary education, and as things stand at present, will struggle to find appropriate employment or have any chance of owning their own homes in the foreseeable future. The chances of them having an adequate pension are vanishingly small, and they face the huge challenges of political turmoil and climate meltdown. How unjust is all of that?

As individuals all we can really do to ameliorate their plight is to help them out in whatever ways we can. It is said that in Britain the Bank of Mum and Dad is the biggest lender/sponsor helping young people to finance their university studies or to aspire to home ownership, and undoubtedly many parents, grandparents and other older relatives are providing child care that would otherwise be cripplingly expensive. Even so, there is grave injustice and young people may well come to the conclusion that they are side-lined from the general march of progress that their parents took for granted.

The monarch butterfly weighs less than a gram, but it makes a migratory journey of over 9000 kilometres, from Mexico to Canada and back. How is this possible? How long would such a journey take? The answer is about four or five butterfly lifetimes, and it is only possible because of a rather wonderful inter-generational relationship.

The butterfly journey is like relay race. The first generation of monarchs sets out from Mexico to fly to a particular known stopover point. There the females lay their eggs and die. The eggs hatch and go through the metamorphosis from caterpillar to chrysalis to butterfly until they are ready to resume the journey. This continues from one settling point to the next, each generation passing on the baton of life to the next and then letting go. What does this teach us about the way we view succeeding generations?

The journey depends on each generation surrendering control when their time comes and trusting the next generation to continue the journey faithfully, but in their own way. The route followed by the second generation will be completely different from that taken by the first. How foolish it would be if the first-generation butterflies were to insist that the next generation do exactly what their parents did. Each stage of the journey will be different, with different rewards and different challenges, and each generation must find the way for itself. How easy are we, when it comes to trusting our young people to meet the challenges of the future in their own way? And yet each generation carries with it what we could call 'the wisdom of the way'. What do we need to pass on to our young people by way of wisdom for the way and what do we need to leave to their own insights and experience?

If we get it wrong, our young people will rightly tear away in revolt, or burst out in protest, and the energy we all need for the journey will be wasted on futile conflict, like spilled wine. And if *they* get it wrong they may miss important signposts along the way to becoming the best we all can be. The journey will only proceed as it should if it is an inter-generational undertaking, with each generation contributing fully to the challenge – fully empowered, fully supported, fully trusted and fully respected.

Pause ...

... to ask for the grace to learn from those who have gone before us and to trust those who will follow after us.

FRIDAY

The heights of hypocrisy

*'Alas for you, scribes and Pharisees, you hypocrites! You pay
your tithe of mint and dill and cumin and have neglected the
weightier matters of the Law – righteousness, mercy, good faith!
… Blind guides, straining out a gnat and swallowing a camel! …
You hypocrites! You clean the outside of cup and dish and leave
the inside full of extortion and intemperance. …You hypocrites!
You are like whitewashed tombs that look handsome on the
outside, but inside are full of the bones of the dead and every kind
of corruption. In just the same way, from the outside you look
righteous, but inside you are full of hypocrisy and lawlessness.'
(Matthew 23:23-28, abbreviated)*

In our times, truth itself has been compromised. Perhaps
truth was always under threat, but in our times that threat
has come out into the open and named itself. It calls itself
fake news, alternative facts, post-truth. These are all false
identities. Its real name is what it always was – lies. One of the
most frightening aspects of this development has been the fact
that lies and deception are openly practised, and therefore
endorsed and legitimised, by those who hold the highest office.
Their example has been eagerly embraced by those who find
more profit in dishonest than in honest dealings. In our times
we face the huge challenge of forces that are erasing the line
between truth and falsehood and rendering every aspect of
the information on which we base our choices untrustworthy.

Jesus meets it head-on, as he confronts the scribes and
pharisees in this unforgettable eruption of righteous anger.

The fracture between truth and falsehood seems to open

up when there is a mismatch between our inner self and our outward dealings. It is the basis of hypocrisy. The agendas that cause this to happen have not changed much through the ages. Self-interest, the interest of the tribe, party or institution, take precedence over the greater good, so that politicians are motivated mainly by what is most likely to get them re-elected, and powerful organisations sacrifice integrity to maintain the outward image and apparent stability of the institution itself, even to the extent of covering up serious abuses and corrupt practices. It's not a pretty picture and we feel helpless to do much about it.

Jesus spells out graphically how hypocrisy serves the outward appearance and neglects the inner demands of truth and justice. I was reminded of this episode when having a meal with friends. It was summertime and the windows were open. A wasp flew into the room along with several flies. A couple of children in the gathering began to panic about the wasp, running around to try to keep out if its way and asking the adults to kill it. Meanwhile the hostess fetched cloths to cover the food. When asked why she was doing this, yet was so calm about the wasp, she explained:

'You panic about the wasp, but the worst it can do is give you sharp sting. It will hurt you for a short while but, unless you are allergic, it won't do you any lasting harm. The flies, on the other hand carry disease on their bodies and when they alight on the food they can infect it. You can't see anything, but your food has been corrupted and if you eat it you may become very ill. Which insect do you think is the more to be feared, the one that stings you and flies away, or the one that poisons your food without your realising it? That is why I am more concerned about protecting the food than killing the wasp.'

Jesus makes it very clear here that outward appearances can be very deceiving, and what really matters is whether the heart is pure. If we apply this logic to some of the people in public office we may want to revise the way we exercise our votes. An even more stringent test is what happens if we apply it to ourselves. How does the image we show to the world match up with what we are truly like inside? How would we feel if we knew that other people were not only able to see our faces and hear our words but could also read our minds?

A good friend of mine, who had published a number of books that had helped many of his readers to find their way along a spiritual path, was dying of cancer. The process of dying took nine months, very significantly, because his true inner self was coming more and more to birth during those months. One of the last things he said, as he looked along the shelf that contained the books he had written was this: 'If only I could *live* what I have written.' I echo that prayer every time I see a book with my own name on the spine.

But lest we get tempted to take ourselves too seriously, let's also not overlook Jesus' ability to make a point by sending up the ridiculous side of human life. I can so imagine the pedantic pharisees counting out the thyme and cumin, the perfect excuse for having no time left for justice and mercy, and as for scrupulously filtering the gnats out of the water then using it to wash down the camels … Let no one suggest that Jesus had no sense of humour.

Pause …

… to ask for the grace to live our true lives and not merely pretend to do so.

SATURDAY

The precipices of change

*Jesus left that place and withdrew to the region of Tyre
and Sidon. And suddenly out came a Canaanite woman
from that district. She started shouting, 'Lord, Son of David,
have mercy on me. My daughter is tormented by a demon.'
But he said not a word in answer to her. And his disciples went
and pleaded with him, saying, 'Get rid of her, for she keeps
shouting after us.' He said in reply, 'I was sent only to the
lost sheep of the House of Israel … It is not right to take the
children's food and throw it to dogs.' She said, 'Yes, Lord; but
even dogs eat the scraps that fall from their masters' table.'
Then Jesus answered her, 'Woman, great is your faith.
Let your desire be granted.' And from that moment her
daughter was well again.
(Matthew 15:21-28)*

One of the biggest challenges in our lives, especially in the current turmoil, is the challenge of change. Change in fact is the only constant in life. Change is happening all the time, from the shedding and renewal of every cell in our bodies, to the struggle to keep up with technological advances. The challenge of change runs right through the gospels too. There are several stories of people who longed for change that never seemed to come. A woman with a persistent haemorrhage had waited twelve years and consulted various doctors but found no relief. A man who had been sitting beside the Pool of Bethesda for thirty-eight years in the hope of a cure. Through Jesus' intervention both are enabled to change their story. But in today's reading it is Jesus himself who is confronted by the challenge to change the story.

The Canaanites were historic enemies of Israel, and here is one of them daring to approach Jesus and ask for help. yet Jesus seems to ignore her request. Even when his disciples urge him to do as she asks, to put a stop to her persistent badgering, he declines, pointing out that he has been sent only to the children of Israel. But the woman won't take 'No' for an answer. Whatever Jesus' reasons may be, and there are several suggestions by commentators, it is clearly the case that this woman's challenge forces him to change his view, from a relatively narrow, even tribal perspective to a more universal one.

It can be painful to have our perspective changed. Usually it takes some external intervention to shift our worldview. Someone says something or our circumstances change and suddenly the old assumptions and certainties don't hold any more. The time has come to change the story. Stories can, and do, go out of date. What seemed beyond question during an earlier stage of our lives now suddenly or gradually looks irrelevant or even simply wrong. Growth always brings change, and change can help us to grow. This incident seems to have been a growth point in Jesus' own journey. It appears that in his times as in ours, the agenda, or the narrative can only be changed by causing a degree of disturbance, which will at the very least produce an awkward tension if not a hostile situation, forcing people to think more deeply about the issue being confronted.

I was in Ireland at the time Queen Elizabeth II made a state visit there in 2011. It could have been a tense occasion given the history, and the still very fresh memories of abuses and atrocities inflicted on the Irish by the British. Instead it was a runaway triumph for change. As head of a constitutional monarchy the sovereign is not permitted to make any kind of political statement and certainly not a formal apology. At a state reception given in her honour in Dublin Castle she made an after-dinner speech in which she expressed regret for 'things we wish had been done differently, or not done at all'. It was a game-changing moment. Her words were so understated, but her meaning was abundantly clear to the Irish who understand nuanced language better than most, and were receptive to it. I will never forget the warmth of feeling that was expressed over the next following days in the streets, pubs and living rooms of the Republic of Ireland. The story had been radically and permanently changed because those involved had the courage to embrace the challenge and to do so with grace and humility.

Are there any stories that need changing in your own life, things from which it is now time to move on? Is our nation's story in need of change, from narrow nationalism towards an open internationalism? How does the world's story need to change, for example to share Earth's resources more equitably and actively work to combat climate change. Where do you see evidence that this change of story is already happening? In what ways does it need to change more?

Pause ...

... to ask for the grace to recognise which stories need to change and the courage to *become* the change we long to see.

SABBATH PAUSE
Dreams and visions

After this I shall pour out my spirit on all humanity
Your sons and daughters shall prophesy,
Your old people shall dream dreams,
And your young people see visions.'
(Joel 3:1-2)

After all the rock climbing, it's high time for a sabbath pause to reflect on the challenges we have faced and to draw deeply on the promise held out to us in today's reading.

I love this reassurance, that the old people shall dream dreams. Old people certainly do dream dreams, but mostly no one wants to know. And young people shall see visions? Our young people are indeed visionary, and they have not yet internalised the message that visions are only worth pursuing if they generate a profit. My conversations with my young granddaughters convince me that the younger the person, the more vivid the vision, but all too quickly their extraordinary visions are stifled by the grey shroud of the commonplace.

So how has this week been for you? Of the challenges we have considered, which most closely speaks to your condition? What challenges would you want to add, and where do you find any guidance in scripture for surmounting them?

Almost everyone longs for peace in the world. Is there any conflict zone in your own life? Can you see any way of reducing the tension at all, perhaps by means of personal contact that helps you recognise the vulnerability of the other person? How would it feel to have a personal conversation with someone with whom you have serious political or theological differences?

Do you ever feel 'all over the place', perhaps about personal matters or maybe you lie awake at night unable to see any way forward in the problems that surround us nationally or globally? Can you relate to the anger and bewilderment of the Gerasene demoniac? Can you let Jesus come alongside you in your confusion?

How do you feel about the inevitable diminishments that accompany the process of ageing? Is diminishment always to be seen as loss, or could it be a way of stripping away the outer layers of our lives in order to come closer to the treasure at the heart of who we truly are?

Would you agree that there is a considerable imbalance between the relatively secure life experience many of us enjoyed in earlier years and the uncertainties with which our young people now have to live? How might we help to reduce this injustice?

How do you feel about the breakdown of trust in our times, and the erasing of the line between truth and falsehood? How could we help our young people, especially, to distinguish between genuine information and manipulative propaganda? If we fail in this, we make ourselves extremely vulnerable to devastating consequences, as history has taught us all too clearly in the 20th century.

Times are changing, rapidly. We struggle to keep up, and we can feel overwhelmed by the rate of change. On the other hand, we sometimes wait in vain for longed-for change to happen, for improvement in some chronic condition or hope in problematic situations. Sometimes we need to change the story, or move on from ways of doing or seeing things that no longer work. How do you feel about the challenge of change?

As we scaled the rockfaces of the challenges we met this week, the motivation was always to come a little closer to the best we can be. This is our vision – the dream that human life can be so much more than we can at present imagine. Many others have embraced this vision before us. One amazing visionary was Nelson Mandela. During the Rivonia Trial in 1964, charged with the capital offence of engaging in militant action, he declared the freedom of his people to be 'an ideal I hope to live for and see realised. But, my Lord (addressing the judge), if it needs to be, it is an ideal for which I am prepared to die.'

We might also be able to name an ideal for which we hope to live – we have explored some examples this past week – the dream of peace, the dream of justice, the dream of a world where truth and integrity trump lies and deception – but which of us could honestly claim that we are prepared if necessary, to die for that ideal?

As we venture into the final week of our journey, we join one who both lived for and died for the vision that fired his whole life: Jesus of Nazareth. We will accompany Jesus on the final week of his own earthly journey and see how he scaled his own rockfaces of apparently impossible challenges. At their best, our own visions and dreams are human reflections of the divine dream – to enable humanity to evolve spiritually to the very best we can be, where we will truly reflect the glory of God.

Endings and Beginningss

MONDAY

Unbinding

Jesus was distressed in spirit, and profoundly moved.
He said, 'Where have you laid him?' They said, 'Lord,
come and see.' Jesus wept, and the Jews said, 'See how
he loved him!'… Again inwardly distressed, Jesus reached the
tomb: it was a cave, closed by a stone. Jesus said, 'Take the
stone away.' …When he had said this, he cried in a loud voice,
'Lazarus, come out!' The dead man came out, his feet
and hands bound with strips of material, and his face
wrapped in a cloth. Jesus said to them,
'Unbind him, let him go.'
(John 11:33-35, 38-39,43-44)

The traditional prelude to the journey through Holy Week, the final week of Jesus' earthly life, is the raising of his friend Lazarus from the dead. Jesus is on his way to Jerusalem, knowing by now what fate awaits him there. He will enter the holy city on a donkey, a ride that we commemorate on Palm Sunday.

But first Jesus responds to an emergency call from his good friends Martha and Mary. Their brother Lazarus is critically ill and they beg Jesus to come and heal him before it is too late. Very surprisingly, Jesus doesn't immediately respond. There is a curious delay, even allowing for the speed of first century communications, between his receiving the message and actually setting out. Martha later blames the death of her brother on this delay and rebukes Jesus resoundingly for it.

Eventually he arrives in Bethany to be told that Lazarus is

dead and buried, and Jesus' grief is obvious. But then he issues three clear instructions that may have much to teach us today. First, he tells the by-standers to 'take the stone away'. Then he instructs Lazarus to 'come out'. And finally, he commands the bystanders to 'unbind him'.

Moving the stone is obviously something that Lazarus can't do for himself, even given that he is alive. This is the first reminder that we need each other. The stone that keeps us trapped in a dead place in our lives can take many forms: low self-esteem, fear of failure or criticism, lack of necessary skills or confidence, or external coercion and oppression. Usually we will need help in shifting stones like this. Maybe you know someone who needs a hand with some stone-shifting?

But then comes the big challenge, to Lazarus, to 'come out'. This is the hard part. When we are stuck in a dead place, it can become a comfort zone. Our fears can keep us locked inside because the new life that is calling us to move on holds so much uncertainty. How will we cope? Do we really want to change direction? This is an instruction that only Lazarus can fulfil. Likewise, only we ourselves can respond to the invitation to 'come out' of the situation of captivity and take the risk of whatever the new life holds. What form does your own 'tomb' take, and what would it mean to you if Jesus were to call you to 'come out'?

And finally, the by-standers are asked to 'unbind' him. At first sight this seems like a very obvious thing to ask. Lazarus is wrapped in a shroud. He can't possibly unbind himself. He needs help. This is simply a practical step to enable Lazarus to resume a normal, mobile life. However, for me this sentence resonates more deeply. The term 'unbind him' translates into German as the verb 'entbinden' which means to give birth. The Entbindungsaal is the Labour Ward. So I always associate this incident with the process of giving birth. Lazarus' release from the tomb is also a kind of birthing into a new life, and like any birthing it needs help. It needs midwives. Jesus calls on those at the scene to help Lazarus bring the new life into the world. In a very real sense we are all engaged in bringing to birth the best human being we can be. Right at the start of our journey together we reflected on Paul's observation that all creation is engaged in a great process of labour, of bringing God's kingdom to birth on planet Earth. Each of us plays a unique part in this process, and all of us need each other.

As we have made this journey, with its obstacles and challenges, we have been experiencing these labour pains for ourselves. But birthing is not all about pain. It yields new life. The joy of the new life far outweighs the anguish of the birthing. To become the person we are created to be there will be pain as well as joy, challenges as well as rewards, but the destiny towards which we strive is beyond anything we can imagine.

Birthing is a process of parturition, and this means letting go. As we move into Holy Week, we see just how much Jesus has to let go as he approaches the cross and the emptiness of the grave. It is the only way that leads to the new life that he promises, and then fulfils in his own person on Easter morning.

Pause ...

... to ask for the grace to help each other remove the stones that block our journey and risk the call to come out of our places of confinement.

TUESDAY

Blood, sweat and tears

*Then Jesus withdrew from them, about a stone's throw
and knelt down and prayed, saying. 'Father, if you are
willing, take this cup away from me. Yet not my will but
yours be done.' Then an angel from heaven appeared to him,
strengthening him. In his anguish he prayed more earnestly,
and his sweat became like great drops of blood falling to
the ground. Standing up from prayer and going to the
disciples he found them sleeping for grief. And he said
to them, 'Why are you asleep?'*
(Luke 22:41-46)

Blood, sweat and not infrequently tears commonly accompany birth, but here we see Jesus struggling with himself and with God over all that is to come – an agonising death. He has asked his friends to 'stay awake' with him, but they have fallen asleep in their utter exhaustion, leaving him alone in his final hours of mental and spiritual torment. Alone, that is, except for an angel who comes to give him strength. Very few of us, thank God, can relate to such an extreme and desperate situation, and yet our soul journeys, too, have their moments when we feel we will break under the pressure of grief or fear or loneliness in our hour of need.

It's the middle of the night in a seriously over-stretched maternity unit in a busy city hospital. A young woman has been admitted in premature labour. She has been in agony for hours now as the contractions have wrenched her last ounce of energy from her. Her partner sits helplessly at the bedside, also worn out by the long vigil and the sound and sight of her suffering. Their child is so very much wanted. They have waited for years for this moment. They have constructed a world of future possibilities around the hope of this baby's arrival. They already know that they are expecting a little girl. She has made it to 21 weeks' gestation. Her chances of survival at this stage are slender. Beads of sweat streak the consultant's face and her demeanour is sombre as the foetal heartbeat wavers. She has been with the patient all day and now all night and she knows that there will probably not be a happy outcome, but she throws all her energy and skill into the effort to save this precious little life. Beside her a trainee student watches and waits and wonders whether a medical career is really what she wants.

Across the street the church clock strikes one. The city sleeps. A broken-hearted couple hold their lifeless baby in their arms, for the first and the last time on earth. The experienced consultant, who has seen so much life and death during her years in the profession, is unable to hold back her own tears. The student turns aside and wonders how the city can sleep so peacefully through so much overwhelming pain. The bereft parents are engulfed in an abyss of sorrow. Where is the visiting angel, to give them strength?

And yet, there *is* an angel. She comes to them quite unexpectedly in the doctor's tears. She comes to them in the vulnerability of another human being who dares to let her own feelings show through the shell of professional detachment. For a moment patient and doctor are one, and in that moment lies just enough strength for both to see the bitter journey through to the end.

Perhaps you have had your own experience of wondering how the rest of the world can continue to function, apparently untouched by a grief that for you is overwhelming. Perhaps you have known times when you couldn't go a single step further along the rocky road, but fell into a desperate and exhausted sleep, and possibly in that sleep the angel came and delivered just enough new strength to keep on walking.

Something like this happened to Elijah in the desert, when

he felt he couldn't go on living. He lay down in his despair, begging God to take his life, and fell asleep. As he slept an angel came and left him a little water and a morsel of food (1 Kings 19:4-8). A morsel is often all the angel brings, but it is enough. And sometimes the angel has our name, and we are called to bring a morsel of strength to another person's pain. It can take so many forms: a gentle word of encouragement, a gesture of compassion, an offer of help, a reassuring hug. So little, it seems, yet just enough to assure the other that we are awake, that we feel with them, that we care.

Where do you find yourself in the Gethsemane of life? Perhaps you are the one in agony. Perhaps you are asleep? Perhaps you are the angel? All of us will be all of these at some point in the journey. When has an angel brought you a morsel of hope or encouragement that enabled you to carry on? Does anyone need a morsel of hope from you right now?

The events of Holy Week will demonstrate that Jesus was at his most powerful when he was at his most humanly vulnerable, helpless on Calvary. Can we trust that our own inner vulnerability may be a greater blessing to others than all our apparent strength? Tears will melt defences that no steel can breach.

Pause ...

... to ask for the grace to stay awake, even in the presence of overwhelming pain and to trust that the greatest strength is often hidden in the deepest human vulnerability.

WEDNESDAY

Candles in the wind

'Someone who has dipped his hand into the dish
with me will betray me.'
'I say to you, this very night, before the cock crows you
will deny me three times.'
Then all the disciples deserted him and ran away.
(Matthew 26:24, 34, 56)

Betrayed, denied, abandoned … this is Jesus' experience of the friends he has chosen to carry his vision forward. He has spent his years of public ministry kindling the fire of the gospel in the hearts of these chosen ones, but when the storms blow up, the candles flicker and go out. Candlelight is fragile, and Jesus initially entrusts his entire mission to twelve flimsy candles.

One of them, someone who has shared the same dish at table, will actually hand him over to the authorities and to a terrible death. If you consider your own circle of close friends, how would it feel if one of them betrayed you so cruelly?

Another, who has vowed undying loyalty and solidarity with Jesus, whatever may happen, and has declared himself willing to die with him and for him, now denies ever having known him, and does so three times, when it becomes clear that to admit to knowing Jesus could expose him to the same fate.

And as for the rest of the chosen team, well, when the chips are down they are off, running for their lives, leaving their friend to his fate.

But as in all things, it's very easy to point a finger of

criticism, and much harder to face how we ourselves would have behaved in the circumstances. In a leafy middle-class residential area of a large European city, as I read just today, ordinary citizens are being targeted by the far right because of their vocal resistance to neo-Nazi politics. One woman who simply refused to take a campaign leaflet from a far-right candidate had her car torched and her windows smashed. Not many of us would stand firm in the face of this kind of threat and how greatly these valiant agents of resistance deserve our respect for their civil courage. Yes, I might have denied, I might have abandoned, but I sincerely hope I would not have betrayed Jesus.

Yet these men were the first team, the premier league. It is their statues that adorn our cathedrals, they who get their saint's days and have churches named after them. They are the ones we remember – the candles that went out when the storm blew up.

However, there were others, with names we can hardly remember or no names at all – little people who came out of their obscurity when it was most dangerous to do so – people who spoke up for Jesus in word or gesture when he desperately needed it. They are the B team, and they don't get any lasting memorial, and barely a mention in the script. They are 'extras', with only a brief walk-on part in the drama of Jesus' last week on earth.

I think of the women who stood faithfully at the foot of the cross, holding vigil for the loved and dying one, unafraid of the consequences, because their love and their grief was greater than their fear. Their faithfulness is reflected again and again in those who hold vigil for sick and dying loved ones everywhere, maintaining silent solidarity when it matters most.

There was the nameless person who led the disciples to the secret upper room where they could celebrate Passover in relative safety, and the unknown person who made that room available to them. There was the centurion, in the pay of the Romans, who had the courage to acknowledge the terrible mistake they were making. There was the legendary

Veronica who wiped Jesus' face with her cloth as he made his way to Calvary, and who stands for all those who lined the streets that day and reached out in compassion. There was the person who offered Jesus vinegar on a sponge, in an effort to ease his thirst and his pain.

We will meet more of them as we continue this week's journey – fragile candles whose light was kindled by coming close to Jesus, and that the wind of opposition could not blow out.

We can't identify with the first team. They have been perched too high for too long on their plaster pedestals in the church. Now worshippers light candles at the feet of those whose light flickered and failed when the wind blew too hard. But we can identify with the 'little people' who brought their own tiny flame into the darkness, because our own flame is also tiny and our darkness deep, and we will never make the spiritual premier league, but it was the reserve team who were there for Jesus when it really mattered.

Pause ...

... to ask for the grace to keep our candle burning and trust that no storm can extinguish the flame of love.

THURSDAY
Costly friendship

*As they were leading Jesus away they seized on a man,
Simon from Cyrene, who was coming from the country,
and laid on him the cross to carry behind Jesus.*
(Luke 23:26-27)

I often wonder how Simon of Cyrene felt when he was forcibly conscripted to help carry Jesus' cross. I discovered one possible answer from a young woman I once met. She had been married for just a short time when her husband was involved in an accident that left him partially paralysed and in need of constant care. She told me how she had felt that her own life had been hi-jacked by the accident. For the rest of their life together she would be her husband's carer. All the plans they had made were shattered. Life would never ever be the same. It was easy to understand that she felt a degree of resentment at the unexpected turn her life had taken.

It happened, however, that she came across the incident with Simon of Cyrene one day as she was meditating on scripture. His story immediately resonated with her own, and she tried to enter imaginatively into the scene. As she did so she found herself, in her prayer, being forced to carry another's cross, and she also discovered that of all the people who encountered Jesus on his last day on earth, Simon of Cyrene was the person who came closest to him. This insight gave her new strength and a sense of purpose that I hope she was able to draw on as the years moved on for them both.

Another person who emerges out of obscurity to stand in solidarity with Jesus is Joseph of Arimathea, who approaches the authorities for permission to take Jesus' body and bury it in a fresh-hewn grave. To do this for someone convicted of alleged subversion against the state demanded a huge degree of courage. Just imagine doing it today for someone your nation has convicted of being a threat to national security. Joseph does not hold back, and his request is granted.

As soon as the Passover festival is over, Jesus is tended by another faithful friend, Mary of Magdala, who carefully observes where he is to be buried and goes as soon as she can to that place to anoint his broken body. She has never wavered in her companionship. She is the first person to learn of his resurrection and becomes the first apostle, sent out to announce the good news.

These companions on Jesus' final journey remind me of a story about a man whose friend gave him a brand-new sports car. One day he was driving through a very deprived part of town and had to park the car in the street. When he returned he noticed a scruffy looking street kid walking round his new car. 'Don't you touch my car,' he called out, and the boy turned and asked him: 'What a fantastic car. Where did you get it?' 'My friend gave it to me actually,' the man replied. 'Wow,' said the boy, 'I wish I could ...' and the man finished off his sentence for him – 'You wish you could have a friend like that?' 'No,' said the boy, thoughtfully. 'I was going to say I wish I could *be* a friend like that.'

Simon, Joseph and Mary are friends like that, coming alongside Jesus when the chips are down. Each of them is identified not just by name but by their place of origin: Simon, from Cyrene; Joseph, from Arimathea; Mary, from Magdala. But there is a fourth B team player who is given neither name nor place of origin. He is the thief who is crucified at Jesus' side. He makes no attempt to conceal or excuse his guilt. He honestly acknowledges that his punishment is deserved, but that Jesus is innocent. He doesn't ask for any miraculous release from his own cross but prays simply 'Jesus, remember me, when you come into your kingdom.' Rarely could there have been so heartfelt a prayer, and one that has re-echoed countless times through the ages. This isn't just a plea to be kept in mind, but the expression of a deep desire to be re-membered, to have our fractured hearts put together again and made whole.

The so-called penitent thief is not named; he stands for everyone. His origin is not specified; he comes from everywhere. We can insert our own name for his, our own home ground for his, and we too can hear Jesus' response. 'Truly I tell you, today you will be with me in Paradise.'

Perhaps one or other of these unlikely companions of Jesus' final hours speaks to your heart in a special way. If so, you might like to enter more deeply into their story in imaginative meditation and discover what insight it gives you into your own journey. Or, as you reflect on the account of Jesus' suffering and death, you might find other 'extras' in the drama who show you something of yourself and your situation. Who is the 'Jesus' right now in your own neighbourhood who desperately needs someone to offer authentic friendship? How might you respond to that need? How might you be the friend that the boy in the story so longed to be?

Pause ...

... to ask for the grace to be the friend who stays faithful when friendship becomes costly.

GOOD FRIDAY
Out of the depths

Out of the depths I cry to you, O Lord;
Lord, hear my voice. (Psalm 130:1)

From noon onwards there was darkness over all the land
until mid-afternoon. And at that time, Jesus cried out in a loud
voice, 'Eli, eli, lama sabachthani?' that is, 'My God, my God,
why have you forsaken me?'
(Matthew 27:45-46)

This has to be the most desolate moment in the gospels. Jesus has been betrayed, denied and abandoned by those he had trusted to walk with him, through the valley of the shadow of death, and now he feels forsaken even by God. This is his ground zero, and perhaps we too have our own experiences of ground zero. How did it come to this?

This moment of total aloneness in the midst of a terrible meltdown is the climax of a process of being stripped down to the very core of existence. It reminds me of the sets of Russian dolls, where first the outermost doll is taken away, to reveal a slightly smaller doll inside, and so the process continues through four or five layers, until just a tiny doll is left. When I reflect on these dolls I see in that tiny remaining doll an image of what we might call the core of our being – all that remains when everything else is stripped away.

In these last days of his life Jesus is first stripped of the comfort and security of faithful friendships as one after another of his friends lets him down. Then he is stripped of any trust he might have had in the judicial system, as he is condemned by the kangaroo courts of ecclesiastical and political authority. Then he is stripped of his human dignity, mocked, scourged and exposed to full public view as a convicted 'enemy of the state'. And now the fourth stripping – the loss of trust even in God's promise. Soon will follow the final stripping – the loss of life itself.

However, in the heart of the nest of dolls lies the one tiny doll that cannot be broken down any further. The core of our being is indestructible, even though we can't imagine such a possibility when we are in the throes of the stripping down. I was once in a desolate state of my own, unable to see my way through a thicket of what seemed to be insoluble problems. I had a little vase of sweet peas on my desk at the time, and as the days went by I grew more and more disheartened as these lovely flowers lost their petals, one by one. I knew that the time was fast approaching when they would be gone, and I would have to return to the problems still waiting for my response. One evening I noticed that the final petals had fallen, and my own tears began to fall too. I went up close to the dead blooms, and only then did I see the beautiful, pure white seedpods that remained, only becoming visible when the flowers had died. The seed of the future was indestructible.

Reflecting back over this experience, and, especially, over Jesus' own experience of feeling the loss of even his Father's presence, leads me to wonder what this last stripping means for me, and possibly even meant for Jesus. For me it is the loss of *certainty*. Like many pilgrims I have walked long miles of faith using an inherited map of certainty. The rules and doctrines I was taught were presented as being fixed and certain and if I had my doubts it had to be me who was in error. Certainty on the soul journey can easily become a cul-de-sac, and once we settle there we will readily buy into the illusion that we have 'arrived'. If that happens, the journey ends and we will stop growing.

But then comes that point along the journey when our certainties begin to unravel. Is all we have been taught really from God, or has it been invented or at least severely edited, by human hands? We begin to ask who God is for us, and what it all really means. Our whole image of God may crumble. And only then will we realise that this is what it was, just our own flawed *image* of God and not the reality of the universal mystery. This phase of our journey feels like ground zero, but today's reading reminds us that Jesus himself was stripped of this last and most crucial of all certainties – the certainty about Godself.

Certainties can fall away like the petals on my sweet peas. The miracle is that when all the certainties have withered and died, only then do we get a glimpse of what we really long for and can perhaps only describe as pure *mystery*, held invisibly in the seedpod.

From this point our soul journey proceeds in a fog – a fog that the mystics call the cloud of unknowing. Today we remember that Jesus walks through this fog along with us. If we dare to continue the journey we will find that our surrender of certainty is not the devastating loss we feel it to be, but a gift. It is, however, a gift wrapped in a crown of thorns, and a joy that only grows on the other side of sorrow. It is a gift which, when unwrapped, will open the road to a mystery infinitely greater than the sum total of all our human certainties.

Pause ...

... to ask for the grace to let go of our imagined certainties to make space for sacred mystery.

HOLY SATURDAY
Inside the chrysalis

When it was evening, there came a rich man of Arimathea,
called Joseph, who had himself become a disciple of Jesus.
This man went to Pilate and asked for the body of Jesus.
Then Pilate ordered it to be handed over. So Joseph took
the body, wrapped it in a clean linen cloth, and put it in
his own new tomb which he had hewn in the rock.
He then rolled a large stone to the doorway of
the tomb and went away.
(Matthew 27:57-61)

The utter aloneness and abandonment of Jesus' last hours, the loss of everything including even the felt sense of the presence of God, now gives way to a different kind of emptiness, as his body is placed in Joseph of Arimathea's new tomb. Today is a time of enforced inaction and helplessness. It is the nameless gap between Good Friday and Easter Sunday, the space we don't quite know what to do with. For many it is merely the space between the hot cross buns and the Easter eggs, but if we enter into Holy Saturday as fully as we dare, we may find that it is the most important time of all, and we may be invited to spend 'tomb time' of our own.

How might it be, to bury all our own hopes and dreams in the darkness and emptiness and let that stone be rolled across the entrance, blocking the last hope of release? Perhaps there have been periods in your soul journey that felt like this? If so, let today's reflection be an invitation to risk what might seem like annihilation, trusting only in the promise that the seed has to fall into the earth and disintegrate before the new life can emerge from it. The tomb is a terrifying place, but it is also that infinitely beautiful white seedpod that is left when all the petals have fallen from the flower. In the very epicentre of death there is the seed of new life.

This may sound like wishful thinking – just another religious platitude – were it not for the fact that the entire natural world proclaims the same truth. Life on earth exists because of the cataclysmic death of first-generation stars that released into the universe the elements of which physical life is formed. More accessible to our observation is the butterfly's story. The cells that will form the various components of the mature butterfly, known as the imaginal cells, are already present in the egg and all through the caterpillar stage, during which their development is suppressed by the caterpillar's immune system until the time is right for them to become active.

The miracle happens in the chrysalis, but only after the caterpillar has disintegrated into a gooey soup that looks nothing like a caterpillar and nothing like a butterfly. It is a very real process of dying, and it is the only way the future butterfly can evolve. Only when the caterpillar has been completely broken down and the resistance of its immune system has definitively failed, can the imaginal cells come together to form the butterfly. The chrysalis stage is the place – the only possible place – where the transformation can happen, and the beautiful creatures, the monarchs and red admirals, the painted ladies, peacocks and swallowtails that visit our summer gardens can come into being.

The tomb is a chrysalis. Jesus' time in the tomb is the time during which his physical presence is transformed into the energy of the Holy Spirit. Our time in the tombs we have to visit as we make our soul journey are also potentially time and space for a personal experience of transformation. Change happens when we are helpless to resist it. New directions emerge when the former tracks of our lives become so entangled that they are no longer viable. The infinite possibilities of the sacred mystery begin to show through the fog only when we have shed our human and very limited 'certainties'. The delicate colours of possibility begin to become visible through the haze of our unknowing just as the colours of the future butterfly begin to show through the thin membrane of the chrysalis.

On our soul journey the tomb can mean many things: a time of hopelessness when our most cherished hopes and dreams fall apart; a time of enforced immobility, either physical, mental or emotional; a time of grief and letting go of a beloved person or valued relationship. Perhaps these are all dress rehearsals for the final tomb when we, like Jesus, let go of life itself, slipping into the darkness of a mystery we cannot begin to understand, but that we are invited to trust – all the way, the seemingly endless way, to the place of resurrection.

The waymarks along this final week of our journey, and the final week of Jesus' life, all seem to point towards endings – the end of friendships, the end of our own resources, the end of our own certainties, the fading of the light, but they have also offered us hints of new beginnings – the discovery of unexpected friendships and directions, and new growth, germinating invisibly in the depths of our experience.

Tomorrow those new beginnings take us back to where we first began, but no longer the pilgrims we were when we set out.

Pause ...

... to ask for the grace to trust the power of the chrysalis, the fullness held inside the emptiness, the possibility inside every apparent impossibility.

EASTER SUNDAY
Back to Galilee

The angel spoke; and he said to the women,
'Do not be afraid. I know you are looking for Jesus,
who was crucified. He is not here, for he has been raised,
as he said. Come and see the place where he lay, then go
quickly and tell his disciples, "He has been raised from the
dead and see, he is going ahead of you to Galilee; there
you will see him."'
(Matthew 28:5-7)

The journey of Holy Week ends not in a distant destination, but in a journey back to where it all began. Jesus of Nazareth has been transformed, in the darkness and emptiness of the chrysalis, into the Spirit of the risen Christ. No wonder then that the women can't find him in the place where they expect him to be. He has passed from Somewhere to Everywhere, and the angel instructs them to go back to Galilee. Perhaps if the angel had encountered Simon he would have directed him back to Cyrene, or Joseph back to Arimathea, or Mary back to Magdala. Where would he have directed *you*?

Our soul journey is not about arriving anywhere else, but about returning to the places where we work and play, live and love, and seeking to transform our human situations and relationships through the choices we make, inspired now by a Spirit infinitely more powerful than we can ask or imagine. The angel's promise assures us that wherever 'Galilee' is for us, the risen Christ will go there ahead of us, and we will see the power of his transformative presence in ways that we had not recognised until now.

We have been on a six-week journey, a spiritual pilgrimage along a path that has taken us through very different kinds of terrain.

We began by listening to some of the ways in which we are invited to set out on such a journey and noticing our own responses. We gratefully discovered some signposts along the way, warning us of possible pitfalls and suggesting the better paths to choose.

No one promised us that this journey would be a walk in the park, and we soon came up against various obstacles with the potential to drain our energy or deflect us from the true course we are seeking. Then, having paid attention to these obstacles we were rewarded by a phase of the journey that offered us fresh springs of encouragement and places to rest and renew our strength and helped us to keep going.

These oases of encouragement, we discovered, were given so that we might find the courage to meet new and perhaps unprecedented challenges. This stage of our journey comprised several rocky slopes requiring us to look more deeply at some big questions of our times and reflect on how we might address them in our own personal and national lives.

And by this route, over rocks and ravines, punctuated by fresh springs of life-giving water, we arrived at the last week of the earthly life of Jesus of Nazareth, and made the journey of Holy Week alongside him – or rather we walked our own *via dolorosa* with Jesus alongside *us*. It was a walk that brought us not to some glittering heaven, but to a dark and lonely grave, where we were shown the greatest miracle of all. Amid the broken shards of what seemed like so many endings, a whole new beginning unfurled out of the grave-clothes left neatly folded by the buried Jesus as his eternal reality emerged into the risen Christ.

It doesn't matter whether or not this mysterious process took three days in human time because its eternal reality is an ongoing miracle of transformation that calls each of us to engage with it in our own circumstances. It doesn't matter that history records it as an event that occurred two thousand years ago among a particular group of people, because the ever-present mystery challenges us to active participation, whoever and wherever we are, in the continuous task of becoming the best version of humanity, individually and collectively, that we can possibly be.

And now the final signpost directs us back to our start point, but it isn't just a circular route. It is a spiral journey, and in every choice we make along the way we either rise a little closer to the best we can become, or we regress a little. The direction in which we move, both personally and as a community, a nation, and a human race, depends on our day-by-day, moment-by-moment choices as we strive to respond to what Love is asking of us.

Go back now to your Galilee, blessed and enlightened by the dawning of Easter, and make it a place where the Holy Spirit makes her dwelling place, joining all our endings and beginnings in a sacred circle of wholeness and of love.

Looking back

At the end of our pilgrimage we are standing, we might say, at the top of the mountain we thought, six weeks ago, was impossible to climb. Now we can look back over the journey and see the surrounding landscape – the landscape of our lives – from a different viewpoint. We can see fields of our experience that have flourished and borne fruit, and others that appear to have failed. We have gained a wider vision: what we once regarded as our successes are not now seen as triumphs, nor are our failures seen as disasters. We can see that our lives comprise many fields, and that last year's failed crop can become nourishment for next year's growth.

We have also discovered that a journey for which we have no map and for which there is no pre-defined path nevertheless leads us closer to our desire to become the best we can be. And now the challenge is to go *down* the mountain, bringing the insights we have gained back to the valley, where our lives are actually lived.

We do not return to the valley the same people as when we set out. Every encounter along the way changes us, bringing us a little closer to our best self, or causing us to slip a little further from it. And so we bring back to the valley of everyday life the fruits of this particular journey, to nourish us through the coming months and to share with those with whom we share our lives. There will be other journeys, other calls to climb other mountains, and we will be a little better prepared to meet the next challenge for having faithfully faced the last.

We take one final look back over the path we have walked so far, and for its blessings we say 'Thank you!' We turn our eyes to the valley below, with its unknown future demands and expectations, and to these we say 'Yes!'

SUPPLEMENT
Approaches to prayer

Lectio Divina – **The Prayer of the Listening Heart**

This method of prayer was used in early Christian times, when very few people could read. The *lectio*, although it means *reading*, originally meant listening with an open heart to the words of scripture being read aloud to them. As they listened, they were invited to notice anything that especially spoke to them, and then to take it away and chew it over in their cells.

To practise *lectio divina* yourself, begin by reading a piece of scripture slowly and thoughtfully, noticing any phrase, or image that stirs you in some way. There is no need at this stage to ask why this particular phrase is speaking to you, or to try to analyse your reaction. Your subconscious mind is registering an interest in this word or image before your conscious mind has had a chance to get in the way. Simply notice what is happening inside you and receive it as a gift. If you feel moved to do so, let this prayer lead into a conversation with God, or just stay a while in the sacred silence. Don't worry if nothing specially comes to mind. Simply spending time like this with scripture is itself a source of grace.

As your day moves on, whenever there is a quiet moment bring your phrase or image to mind and chew it over. Where and how does it connect to the lived reality of your everyday life? Is it speaking to you in some personal way, perhaps challenging or affirming you in some way? This kind of deep listening automatically leads you to reflect on your experience, and to respond to it, in ways that live on long after the time of prayer itself is over.

Entering into the Gospel in imaginative prayer

Your imagination can be the place where two worlds meet: the world of Gospel truth and the world of your daily life. Here are some suggestions for entering into the Gospel stories and becoming a part of what you see and read.

- Choose a Gospel story that especially appeals to you. Read the passage through slowly, maybe several times and then relax and let yourself imagine the scene. Don't try to stage-manage it, but just let your imagination suggest the scene to you spontaneously in a personal way.

- Use your senses. What can you see, hear, smell, taste or feel? What is the weather like? What is happening in the scene? Is anyone else there? Anyone you recognise? What kind of atmosphere does the scene suggest?

- Now let the action of the scene unfold. Where do you find yourself in the scene? Perhaps you are one of the crowd, or one of the disciples. Perhaps you feel like an outsider looking in, or you may identify with the person being healed, or challenged, or invited into a new relationship with the holy. Don't make any judgements, or force yourself to be where you think you *ought* to be. The power of this prayer is to recognise the place where you really feel you are, and to let the light of Christ shine upon that place.

- How are you feeling about what is happening in your scene? Disturbed? Attracted? Curious? Afraid? Eager? Just notice and acknowledge your feelings. Don't try to censor them. Do you feel drawn to speak with anyone there? What do you want to say? Do you feel that anything is being said to you? Can you enter into a conversation with Jesus?

- If you have noticed at any point that one part of the scene has brought up especially strong feelings in you (either positive or negative), go back in your imagination to that particular part. Don't force anything, but just ask the Holy Spirit to lead you into what is especially important for you. The feelings you have are coming from deep down, and they have something to tell you. Ask God to help you explore them. Does anything in the scene or the incident connect to something that is going on right now in your own life, or does it perhaps strike some chord in your memory.

- End your time of prayer with an expression of gratitude for this time of being consciously in the divine presence and for anything it may have shown you. Maybe end with a familiar prayer.
- If you feel able to do so, share your experience of prayer with a trusted friend, who understands the nature and power of this kind of personal prayer. As you share something of your experience you will discover more of its meaning for you.

Reviewing the day with God

A conscious review of the events of our everyday lives is the foundation of the habit of reflective living. This ancient practice is traditionally known as the *Examen*, or *Examination of Conscience*. Today, however, most people prefer to see it simply as a review of the day, looking back over the day's events, noticing, and reflecting on where God has been for us, and how our response to that presence has been.

By taking a few minutes at the end of the day (or whatever time works best for you) just to reflect on what has been happening, you can re-connect your outer daily life with your inner soul journey. Here are a few suggestions for making this kind of prayer part of your daily routine. You can, of course, shape and adapt this prayer entirely as you wish.

- Begin by asking for the grace to recognize where the Holy Spirit has been present and active in the events of the day, and to shed sacred light on your own memories and feelings about what has been happening.
- Let the day's events re-play, like a video in fast forward, and just notice anything that particularly catches your attention. Stay with that memory, as if you were pausing the video to look more closely at that part.
- Acknowledge everything you feel grateful for, re-living it in your memory and expressing your gratitude either in words

or in silence. Perhaps there was a meeting with someone, or a letter, or a friendly gesture? Did something make you laugh, or move you to tears? Has a problem been solved, or did you experience something in creation that made you feel joy?

- Remember in your prayer those who deserve your gratitude for the blessings the day has brought: those who provided the food you ate, or the essential services; those who did something for you that they didn't need to do. Remember something in the day that you yourself can be proud of. (We often find this difficult.)

- What happened to energise you or make you feel more fully alive? Were you able to give a sign of love to another person? Did anything drain you of energy or leave you feeling less fully alive?

- What choices did you make today, and how do you feel now about the way you made your choice? Did it add to, or diminish the store of love, hope and integrity in the world?

- Are there any dark patches during the day? Is there something that you now wish you had handled differently? Is there some hurt that you are still carrying? Don't make any judgements, of yourself or of anyone else, but simply express your feelings honestly to yourself and to God. You may feel that the day has been unspeakably awful, and it's OK to say so.

- Is there any unfinished business from the day? Maybe something has left you feeling inadequate or fearful or resentful? Let it rest there in the light of God's love, and ask for the grace of healing and enlightenment.

- Close your prayer by asking for God's continuing blessing upon tomorrow's living, as you let yourself sink more deeply into a holy and eternal presence that means well with you.

* * *

Finally, in all we do and in all that happens, may we live our lives in 'an attitude of gratitude', remembering the wisdom of the thirteenth-century mystic, Meister Eckhart, who said that 'if the only prayer you ever say in your entire life is *thank you*, it will be enough'.

Made in United States
Orlando, FL
23 January 2022